D0264725

THE FOOD & COOKING OF
NORWAY

THE FOOD & COOKING OF
NORWAY

Traditions • Ingredients • Tastes • Techniques • 60 Classic Recipes

Janet Laurence

with photographs by William Lingwood

aqua marine

This edition is published by Aquamarine

Aquamarine is an imprint of
Anness Publishing Ltd
Hermes House, 88–89 Blackfriars Road,
London SE1 8HA
tel. 020 7401 2077; fax 020 7633 9499

www.aquamarinebooks.com;
www.annesspublishing.com

If you like the images in this book and would
like to investigate using them for publishing,
promotions or advertising, please visit our
website www.practicalpictures.com for more
information.

UK agent: The Manning Partnership Ltd,
6 The Old Dairy, Melcombe Road, Bath BA2
3LR; tel. 01225 478444; fax 01225 478440;
sales@manning-partnership.co.uk

UK distributor: Grantham Book Services Ltd,
Isaac Newton Way, Alma Park Industrial
Estate, Grantham, Lincs NG31 9SD;
tel. 01476 541080; fax 01476 541061;
orders@gbs.tbs-ltd.co.uk

North American agent/distributor: National
Book Network, 4501 Forbes Boulevard,
Suite 200, Lanham, MD 20706; tel. 301 459
3366; fax 301 429 5746; www.nbnbooks.com

Australian agent/distributor: Pan Macmillan
Australia, Level 18, St Martins Tower,
31 Market St, Sydney, NSW 2000;
tel. 1300 135 113; fax 1300 135 103;
customer.service@macmillan.com.au

New Zealand agent/distributor: David
Bateman Ltd, 30 Tarndale Grove, Off Bush
Road, Albany, Auckland; tel. (09) 415 7664;
fax (09) 415 8892

Front cover shows Roasted Salmon with
Honey and Mustard (see page 52); page 1
shows Marinated Salmon (see pages 26–7);
page 2 shows Roast Pork Loin with Red
Cabbage (see page 76–7); page 3 shows
Tosca Cake (see pages 122–3).

Publisher: Joanna Lorenz
Senior Managing Editor: Conor Kilgallon
Project Editor: Emma Clegg
Designer: Gabriella Le Grazie
Illustrator: Robert Highton
Photography: William Lingwood
Food Stylist: Fergal Connolly
Prop Stylist: Helen Trent
Production Controller: Don Campaniello

ETHICAL TRADING POLICY

At Anness Publishing we believe that
business should be conducted in an ethical
and ecologically sustainable way, with
respect for the environment and a proper
regard to the replacement of the natural
resources we employ.

As a publisher, we use a lot of wood pulp
to make high-quality paper for printing, and
that wood commonly comes from spruce
trees. We are therefore currently growing
more than 500,000 trees in two Scottish
forest plantations near Aberdeen –
Berrymoss (130 hectares/320 acres) and
West Touxhill (125 hectares/305 acres).
The forests we manage contain twice the
number of trees employed each year in
paper-making for our books.

Because of this ongoing ecological
investment programme, you, as our
customer, can have the pleasure and
reassurance of knowing that a tree is being
cultivated on your behalf to naturally replace
the materials used to make the book you
are holding.

Our forestry programme is run in
accordance with the UK Woodland
Assurance Scheme (UKWAS) and will be
certified by the internationally recognized
Forest Stewardship Council (FSC). The FSC
is a non-government organization dedicated
to promoting responsible management of
the world's forests. Certification ensures
forests are managed in an environmentally
sustainable and socially responsible basis.
For further information about this scheme,
go to www.annesspublishing.com/trees.

© Anness Publishing Ltd 2007

All rights reserved. No part of this publication
may be reproduced, stored in a retrieval system,
or transmitted in any way or by any means,
electronic, mechanical, photocopying, recording
or otherwise, without the prior written permission
of the copyright holder.
A CIP catalogue record for this book is available
from the British Library.

Notes

Bracketed terms are intended for American readers.
For all recipes, quantities are given in both metric and
imperial measures and, where appropriate, in standard
cups and spoons. Follow one set of measures, but
not a mixture, because they are not interchangeable.
Standard spoon and cup measures are level.
1 tsp = 5ml, 1 tbsp = 15ml, 1 cup = 250ml/8fl oz.
Australian standard tablespoons are 20ml.
Australian readers should use 3 tsp in place of
1 tbsp for measuring small quantities of gelatine,
flour, salt, etc.
American pints are 16fl oz/2 cups. American
readers should use 20fl oz/2.5 cups in place of
1 pint when measuring liquids.
Electric oven temperatures in this book are for
conventional ovens. When using a fan oven, the
temperature will need to be reduced by about
10–20°C/20–40°F. Since ovens vary, check with your
manufacturer's instruction book for guidance.
The nutritional analysis given for each recipe is
calculated per portion (i.e. serving or item), unless
otherwise stated. If the recipe gives a range, such as
Serves 4–6, then the nutritional analysis will be for
the smaller portion size, i.e. 6 servings.
Measurements for sodium do not include salt added
to taste.
Medium (US large) eggs are used unless otherwise
stated.

Essex County
Council Libraries

Contents

The Norwegian landscape

Norway is a sensationally beautiful country. There are soaring mountains, peaceful valleys, dark forests, silver lakes, rushing rivers and deep fjords that lead to a coastline fringed with small islands. Some of the highest waterfalls and glacial streams in the world are in Norway. The simple grandeur of nature dominates the country and affects the whole way of life.

In Norway, a short season of long summer days is contrasted with a long season of short winter days. This makes both fishing and farming difficult for much of the year despite the abundance of fish in seas, rivers and fjords and the more temperate climate created by the Gulf Stream. Yet the beauty of the country is indisputable, making such hardships incidental for a population that makes much of the outdoors, all year round. Norwegians fiercely guard their ancient law of allemannsretten, a law which gives everyone the right of access to wild areas. The all-too-short summer is spent out of doors, revelling in days filled with a sun that for much of the country never sets. The long, dark and icy winters, though, require preparation as four to six months of the year see much of the country covered in snow.

The Norwegian attitude to food is deeply bound up in their surroundings and history. Food and cooking traditions can be traced back to the days when maintaining regular food supplies involved ensuring that the short summer harvests yielded enough food to last through the long winters. Despite seasonal extremes, nature is generous in Norway. Both salt and fresh waters teem with high-quality fish. What agricultural land is available is fertile and can be made to produce crops and raise domestic animals. Sheep or goats can feed on green pastures above deep fjords offering a backdrop of dramatic mountains, often with snow-covered peaks, an ever-constant reminder of the short summer season.

Climate

Norway hugs the edge of Scandinavia. A bulb shape in southern and central Norway, the land then stretches and elongates itself up the side of Sweden, over into the top of Finland and then curves over to hug the north of Russia. It is as though the coast of Norway, laced with small islands and fringed with fjords, offers protection to the other northern countries from the blast of the Atlantic. In part this is true. However, the coastal regions are also blessed with the softening effect of the Gulf Stream. Although most of Norway lies on the same latitude as Siberia, it enjoys a much more temperate climate than might be expected, which enables a wider range of crops to be grown.

Over one third of Norway lies within the Arctic Circle, which is the line of latitude linking the places around the world that have at least one full day on which the sun never sets and one day on which it never rises.

Left Soaring mountains provide Norway's fjords with a dramatic backdrop, but limit the amount of land available for agriculture.

As you travel north during the summer, the days when the sun never sets lengthen into weeks. The midnight sun gradually approaches the horizon then, instead of vanishing below it, slowly begins an upward trajectory towards another day. The light around midnight is not quite daylight but has a pearly, mystical quality. Even in southern Norway, the summer sun lingers until almost midnight. Between late May and mid-August, nowhere in the country experiences true darkness.

Endless summer days contrast with polar nights when the sun never rises. Curiously, the periods of sunless days are not as long as those of the midnight sun. And, just as the light at midnight is not that of daylight, so the dark at midday in winter resembles a twilight as if the sun is struggling to break through. Only in a few places in the far north, such as the island of Svalbard, is darkness complete.

Norway offers great variations in both landscape and weather. Most of the country's eastern spine is mountainous, as is the central part of its southern peninsula. Here, winters are bitter and summer temperatures tend to be higher than coastal regions, which have a milder climate with less dramatic extremes between summer and winter. Rain falls generously on some coastal areas, while others have hardly any precipitation – the latter still manage to thrive, due to the many rivers that bring water down from the snow-laden mountains.

The natural landscape

Norway has distinctive natural features in its landscape, which were formed by prehistoric glaciers – mountains, rivers, lakes, waterfalls, glaciers and fjords. The mountain areas typically run from north to south, and consist of plateaus and

Above The shimmering curtains of the Northern Lights, the phenomenon seen in the sky in northern latitudes, are one of the wonders of the Arctic Circle.

Above left Norway's coastline adjoins the Barents Sea in the north, the Norwegian Sea in the west and the southern Skagerrak Strait.

lakes with peaks. Notable ranges include Dovrefjell and Trollheimen in the centre, Jotunheimum in the south and the Kjølen mountain range, which runs throughout most of Norway. Fjords, which are narrow inlets between cliffs or steep slopes with their bases eroded significantly below sea level, characterize the Norwegian landscape and provide spectacularly grand views. The largest fjord is Sognefjorden in the south-west, with other large ones Hardangerfjord, Dragsvik, Nærøyfjord and Geirangerfjord.

Norway: a brief history

Norway's name comes from the Scandinavian words for north, "nor", and way, "vegn". Its history goes back some ten or eleven thousand years. From the Sami through to the Vikings, an independent spirit has reigned and survived not only difficult living conditions but also repeated attempts at domination by the Danes and Swedes. Many have emigrated but those who stayed found countless ways to thrive.

As the last ice age was in retreat, ancestors of the Sami arrived in boats made from the hide of animals or in hollowed tree trunks. These early settlers were nomadic, hunting, fishing and herding. Lacking metal, their tools were made of antler and bone. Seals and whales were hunted with harpoons of bone. These early settlers quickly realized the wealth of food in the sea and that the coastal regions, thanks to the Gulf Stream, had a less extreme climate than other parts of Norway. On land, game was hunted with bows and arrows or with bone javelins. Before long the settlers started tilling the soil as well as domesticating animals.

From those early times, it was obvious that to survive the winter efforts had to be made to conserve food during the summer.

Travel within Norway was always difficult and in winter the terrain made it almost impossible. Building roads over mountains required major effort and winter snows and frosts made roads impassible and destroyed surfaces. Boats became the preferred transport, along coast and rivers and for crossing lakes. In winter, skis were used to traverse snow-covered land.

Early regional kingdoms

Norway first developed as a series of some 29 small kingdoms. A medieval system of masters and serfs operated a seafaring and rural economy. Theirs was a pagan culture. Norwegians have created a rich tapestry of myths and legends, most of which survive to this day. (There is a saying that Norwegians are clever, they know that trolls don't exist. The question is, do the trolls know?) Norwegians believed a host of gods, giants and trolls were an inextricable part of the awesome scenery that surrounded them. Every facet of nature and geography could be ascribed to the actions or characters of one of the mythological creatures that they worshipped.

A scarcity of agricultural land and a practice of taking more than one wife meant men had to go abroad to provide for their families. So, seafaring was in their blood, and life in the mountains and fjords, with the short summers and long winters, had bred a tough race.

The Sami

Previously known as Lapps, the Sami people are an indigenous group who for centuries inhabited the whole of northern Russia, Finland and eastern Karelia. Scandinavian settlers drove them north and, as one of the largest ethnic minorities in Europe, they are still found

Left The Sami of Finnmark, in northern Norway, depend on the reindeer (caribou) for their livelihood and their cuisine.

Right Fish have been hung to dry in Norway and Greenland since medieval times to produce the popular ingredient stockfish.

in Norway, Sweden, Finland and Russia, with over 60 per cent in Norway, largely in the most northern region of Finnmark, where they still herd reindeer (caribou). Their economy has always been based around a strong relationship with the land and its natural resources.

Finnmark has a dual character. Its wild coastline is deeply indented with fjords and scattered with fishing villages, while the interior is a high, broad plateau where the Sami people raise their reindeer. Although Sami ancestors arrived first, others migrated to Scandinavia from central Europe after the ice receded, settling particularly along the southern Norwegian coast. Tall, fair haired, with blue eyes, speaking a Germanic language, these hunter-gatherers may have introduced the fighting instinct that developed into Viking culture.

Vikings

The Vikings set out not only from Norway but also Sweden, Denmark and the Baltic countries. The name Viking comes from vikingar, to pirate. Initially establishing peaceful, farming settlements in Orkney and Shetland off the north coast of Scotland, the adventurous norsemen soon developed powerful boats capable of crossing oceans. Plundering and pillaging, the Vikings ventured far afield, and established themselves in England (King Canute ruled England, Denmark and Norway in the first part of the 11th century) and Normandy in France. From the 9th to the middle of the 11th century, they instilled terror throughout Europe and took possession of a vast horde of riches.

Norwegians have continued to be explorers. Two polar exploration pioneers were Fridtjof Nansen, who crossed the Greenland icecap in 1888, and Roald Amundsen, who reached tthe South Pole in 1911. Then there was Thor Heyerdahl, who made his name by taking the Kon Tiki raft across the Pacific in 1947.

Sustaining the sailors

Viking expeditions would have taken many weeks, during which active sailors needed to be fed large quantities of protein in ships with little storage and few cooking facilities. What made the voyages possible were two of the great culinary discoveries of the Norwegians, dried cod and pickled herring (a rich source of vitamin C, so necessary to avoid scurvy).

To preserve food for winter use, many of the cod that teemed in northern waters were gutted and dried in the wind, first on rocks and then on poles, until they became as hard as a board. Like the South African dried meat known as biltong, bits could then be broken off and chewed, or the whole fish soaked until it

was rehydrated, when it could be cooked. The dried fish was prepared without salt and was known as stockfish. Adding wood ash, or lye, to the boiling water, the Norwegians considerably improved the texture and flavour of the rehydrated fish. The result is the celebrated lutefisk, the taste of which is either adored or abhorred.

By the 6th century, the export of dried fish in exchange for other goods was established. By the 9th century, plants for drying cod had been introduced in Iceland and Norway and the finished product had found a market in northern Europe and the Mediterranean. Later, in the 19th century, the Norwegians perfected a system for salting and drying the cod, the method preferred by the Portuguese (for their bacalhau) and Spanish (for their bacalao), and cooked in many imaginative ways. In Norway, the salted and dried fish was known as klipfish and in fact was more valued as an export than a national delicacy. Until the Spaniards introduced olive oil and tomatoes, klipfish was usually boiled and served with potatoes.

Left Olaf II, known as The Holy, established Christianity as Norway's religion and became the nation's patron saint.

Unification and Christianity

While the Vikings were sailing farther and farther abroad, Harald Fairhair (859–935), the first king of Norway, was conquering and unifying the regional kingdoms at home. After a decisive sea battle in 872 the country became officially united as far north as Trondheim. In practice, however, it remained a country of regions with their own dialects and costumes.

Many of the Vikings who settled in Scotland, England and Ireland converted to Christianity. One of these was Håkon, one of six sons of Harald. Erik, the eldest, murdered four of his brothers, but never suceeded in overcoming Håkon. Erik became king on his father's death but ruled so badly that Håkon came back in 934 to rescue what was left of Harald's achievement. Erik fled to England and managed to take over the throne of York as King Erik Bloodaxe.

So, King Håkon the Good brought Christianity to Norway but neither he nor the new religion survived for long – Håkon was defeated and killed in 960.

It wasn't until Olaf II founded the Church of Norway in 1024 that Christianity was established as the national religion. Known as "The Holy", Olaf became Norway's patron saint. His tomb in Nidaros cathedral in Trondheim was one of the most important pilgrimage destinations in northern Europe.

Despite a period of civil wars, Norway at the start of the 13th century ruled over land from the Isle of Man in the Irish Sea to the Kola Peninsula (now part of the north Russian federation) in the east. In 1262, Greenland and Iceland became Norwegian dependencies. Despite various civil wars, an invasion by Denmark, and trading restrictions in northern Europe, medieval Norway flourished.

Economic change and loss of independence

In the 14th century, the Black Death and other plagues struck in Norway, and this brought a period of economic deterioration. Towns were ruined and land was left uncultivated. Some 80 per cent of the nobility perished along with the feudal system of masters and serfs. From then on Norway was egalitarian and, until the 20th century, its population was primarily rural.

Denmark had long coveted Norway, and from 1537 to 1814 the country lost its independence and became subject to Danish sovereignty. Norway's economy improved gradually during this period, due to careful trade controls of products such as iron, timber and pulp, and by the late 17th century there was a rising generation of wealthy middle classes. The introduction of the potato in the 18th century, easy to grow on a wider range of land than cereals, initiated the development of Norway's rail transport network and signifcantly increased the country's prosperity, in combination with the expansion of herring fisheries on the west coast and the sale of whale, seal and walrus products.

Establishing nationalism

But political control continued to be passed from one country to another. After Napoleon's defeat in 1813, when Denmark and Norway sided with Napoleon against the British and its allies, Norway was ceded to Sweden in the Treaty of Kiel, and its dependencies, Iceland, Greenland and the Faroe Islands, were kept by Denmark. Norway had earlier lost control of the Orkney and Shetland Islands and now its only overseas possession was the uninhabited Bouvet island in the Antarctic.

The growth of trade and increasing prosperity during the 18th century had encouraged feelings of nationalism, further stimulated by the American and

French revolutions. In response to the Treaty of Kiel, and hoping to wrench control of Norway from Sweden, Denmark encouraged an attempt by the Norwegians to gain independence and a national constitution was drawn up on 17th May 1814, still celebrated as their national day.

Throughout the 19th century, Norway's international trade increased, particularly of fish and whale products. Cultural life flourished as the country produced poet and playwright Henrik Ibsen (1828–1906), painter Edvard Munch (1863–1944), and composer Edvard Grieg (1843–1907). Attempts to rescue the language from Danish influence resulted in the creation of a new form of written Norwegian, based on all the various regional dialects.

Still one of Europe's poorest countries, however, emigration increased. In the final three-quarters of the 19th century and the first quarter of the 20th, some 750,000 Norwegians re-settled in North America, nearly as many as remained at home.

Europe and 20th-century prosperity

Norway has long been a seafaring nation with a large merchant fleet. During World War I, despite being neutral, Norway lent Britain considerable aid by delivering essential supplies in return for much needed coal. Neutrality was not maintained in World War II. After the German invasion, King Håkon VII and his government established a government in exile in Britain. Norwegian merchant ships in Allied waters were requisitioned to act as war transports and supply services. By the end of the war, Norwegian naval vessels were fighting alongside the British. After the war, Norway was a founding member of the United Nations.

Towards the end of the 1960s, Norway's economy was transformed by the discovery of oil and gas in the North Sea. From being one of the poorest countries in Europe, it became one of the richest. Successive governments used oil windfalls plus income tax to

Above The ivory tusks of the walrus have always been attractive to hunters. Many were etched and carved by sailors into scrimshaw, products made from marine mammals.

build one of the most extensive social welfare systems in history. Free medical care and higher education, generous pension and unemployment benefits add up to what the government claim is "the most egalitarian social democracy in western Europe". Norway is now ranked as having the highest standard of living in the world, and is also considered to be the most advantageous place for women to live because of its cultural and political freedoms and income equality.

Norwegians today retain their hard-won independence and their deep and abiding love for their country. Almost the whole population has a place in the countryside where they can enjoy rural pursuits: Hiking, fishing, hunting, skiing and seafaring are as important now as they have ever been.

Left Hiking on Djupfjordheia, one of the many outdoor activities that draw not only Norwegians but foreign tourists as well.

Festivals and celebrations

Unsurprisingly, Norwegian celebrations have much in common with those of other Scandinavian countries. One important Scandinavian celebration is the day of Santa Lucia, or the festival of light, which originates in Sweden, with light symbolizing a powerful force that combats the long hours of darkness. Here is a selection of annual holidays and festivities, covering ancient traditions, modern interpretations, as well as more recently introduced festivals.

Festivals can be traced to the changing seasons, the church calendar and historical influences, and range from the very start of the year with New Year's Day, when people's fortunes were predicted, to Christmas, with the traditional key figure of the Norwegian fjøsnisse, or goblin, as well as the more modern figure of Santa Claus.

New Year's Day
This used to be a traditional day of omens when the successful production of crops and food was predicted, as well as the general fortunes of the forthcoming year. It is still an official flag-flying day that is associated with the making of resolutions.

Shrovetide
Fastelavn, or Shrovetide, runs through Shrove Sunday, Shrove Monday (Blåmandag) and Shrove Tuesday or Fat Tuesday (Fetetirsdag), the latter marked by eating a traditional pastry, called semla, filled with marzipan and whipped cream. Officially celebrated on the day before Lent, Shrovetide is also a celebration of the approach of spring.

Easter
The year's most important church festival, Påske, or Easter, is sometimes referred to as the Quiet Week, linked to the Easter message of the suffering of Jesus and his resurrection. Now the celebration has lost much of its sober connotations and provides another occasion for days in the mountains, skiing and celebration. Easter eggs are decorated and rolled down a slope. Easter dishes are typically egg dishes and lamb, the latter originating in the sacrifice of lambs during the Jewish celebration of spring.

Whitsun
Pinse, or Whitsun, in Norwegian means the 50th day after Easter. While less of a tradition, it is still a national holiday.

Constitution Day
Norway's celebration of its independence, also called National Day, falls on 17th May, commemorating the signing of the first constitution in 1814. Breakfast often starts with spekemat (cured meats), smoked salmon, scrambled eggs and pickled herrings, as well as stewed fruits, bread and coffee. In the morning, citizens assemble to greet the king and

Left Constitution Day falls on 17th May. The festival processions include brass bands and school children waving flags.

Women on the northern island of Vardö celebrate Midsummer's Eve by dressing up as witches and dancing around the bonfire.

royal family as they appear on the balcony of the royal palace in Oslo. In other places, the local mayor will stand in for the royal family. Citizens' processions are headed by school brass bands with school children holding Norwegian flags or sprays of newly emerged birch leaves.

Midsummer's Eve

Sankhansaften, Jonsok, or Midsummer's Eve, on 23rd June was an ancient festival to celebrate the summer solstice. On this night, witches were believed to be abroad, plants picked were thought to have healing powers, and bonfires were lit up along the coast to protect against evil spirits. Now Jonsok is a private celebration where people dance around the bonfire.

St Olaf's Day

Olsok, or St Olaf's Day, on 29th July marks the death of King Olaf Haraldsson

Above Children dress up as gnomes at Yuletide on a 19th-century Norwegian farm.

in 1030, who brought Christianity to Norway. An important holy day, traditionally bonfires were lit, especially in rural areas.

All Saints Day

Allehelgens Dag, or All Hallows Day, on 1st November commemorated the Saints, and *Alle Sjeles Dag*, or All Souls' Day, on 2nd November commemorated the dead. 1st November, on the first Sunday in November is now celebrated as All Saints Day, when wreaths and lighted candles are placed on graves. The traditional celebrations are also being influenced by US Halloween customs.

Santa Lucia Day

This custom, which originates in Sweden, is celebrated on 13th December as a feast of light. Dressed in white, young girls wear a crown of lighted candles and offer coffee and buns or cookies.

Christmas

The main Christmas celebration is held on Christmas Eve when it is common to attend carol services. Norwegians use the traditional celebrations of Advent, the

Christmas tree, cards, gifts, and Santa Claus, although there is also the more ancient influence of the Norwegian Fjøsnisse (goblin who lives in the barn), a much-seen symbol at this time of year.

Festive fare varies, but sour cream porridge, usually made with rice and traditionally hiding an almond, is a lunchtime favourite inland. Lutefisk is most often eaten on the coast, where it is a speciality, usually followed by a whole cod. Roast rib or loin of pork is eaten in central and eastern Norway. On the west coast, the traditional dish is pinnekjøtt, smoked and dried lamb ribs.

On Christmas Day there is usually an elaborate koldt bord, or cold table. A Christmas ham studded with cloves or decorated with mayonnaise provides a festive centrepiece, sometimes given extra flavour by being cured in a beer brine before being smoked. The Christmas baking tradition is still strong, and custom used to dictate that seven different kinds of biscuits (cookies) were baked and offered alongside cakes and coffee. What's more, any guest who leaves without eating anything brings bad luck to the house.

The Norwegian cuisine

The food in Norway is defined by its simple, delicate flavours. The traditions of preparing food in this region have always been driven by the practical need to ensure that the produce of the short summer is preserved to last through the long winter. Creative ways of using ingredients, to make them taste good all year round, have been devised and refined ever since the first cod was dried as stockfish to sustain sailors centuries ago.

Above A typical 19th-century Norwegian lunchtime, with porridge and flat bread, shown at the Maihaugen Working Museum.

The Norwegian cuisine derives from its peasant culture, a simple, wholesome diet where food was harvested from sea and land. Families had their own smallholding and it was common for those who lived along the coast to be both fishermen and farmers, with the men fishing and the women running the farm. As a result, the Norwegian diet has been defined by livestock, grain and fish, with plentiful supplies of milk, butter, buttermilk, cheese, meat, bread and fish, particularly cod and herring. Even in contemporary Norway, the emphasis on outdoor activities such as hunting, walking and skiing have ensured that the traditional, sustaining dishes have remained in demand.

Preserving for winter

In Norway, food has always been grown and preserved. Vegetables were selected for their ease of storage, such as beetroot (beet), easily pickled and providing a tasty vegetable accompaniment, and small, plump cucumbers, used to make pickled gherkins. Barley and other grains were great standbys for making sustaining porridge, as well as soups and bread. After the mid-18th century, potatoes appeared and, because they were so easily stored, quickly became an ingrained feature.

Domestic animals (cows, sheep and goats) were fattened on plentiful summer feed and slaughtered in the autumn, when cooler temperatures helped with conservation. Smoking, salting, drying and curing were all traditionally used to preserve meat and fish for winter use.

With the introduction of the cooking stove in the 17th century, oven-prepared dishes shifted the balance from fresh food. However, in modern Norway traditional dishes and cured ingredients –

Right A Fat Tuesday buffet, with yellow pea soup, salted and boiled pork and lamb and smoked sausages with mashed swede.

such as rakefisk, pinnekjøtt and the sour milk cheese gammelost – have once again become popular, in a collective modern nostagia for the traditional patterns of life, as well as a new awareness of the importance of using seasonal produce.

Mealtime traditions

The strong farming heritage dictates that classic dishes are based on local produce. This results in certain regional variations, although the wide availability of all ingredients now makes such differences less marked.

Eating well in the morning was essential for all families to give energy to those working long hours in the open air, and

energy was also needed to stave off the cold brought by the long winters. Frokost, or breakfast, would typically include grøt, a filling porridge that was made by boiling milk with flour, or the richer rømmegrøt, with cream and flour. A sweet version of this is often used for birthdays, summer parties and at Christmas. Breakfast also features cold or cured meats and fish, cheese, eggs, stewed or fresh fruit, fresh and sour milk, and hardbread, with lots of coffee.

Lunchtime has always been a rushed affair, nowadays usually an open sandwich wrapped in special paper called "matpakke" and a very short break of less than half an hour.

The 5 p.m. "middag" for most people is the only hot meal of the day, consisting of a main dish of meat, seafood or pasta, almost always accompanied with potatoes and a small amount of other vegetables.

Dishes for this main meal might include fårikål, a stew with lamb, cabbage and whole peppercorns. In earlier times, this would have been made from mutton, lamb being reserved for the wealthy. Another meat dish is pinnekjøtt, made with cured and sometimes smoked mutton ribs, which is also a favourite for Christmas lunch in the west of Norway. Smalahove is another speciality of the west, made with smoked lamb's head.

Preserved meat and sausages are available in many regional variations, and are typically served with sour cream dishes and flat bread or wheat/potato wraps. Other meat delicacies include an air-dried lamb's leg called fenalår, and mor, a smoked cured sausage.

One of Norway's most recognized fish dishes is smoked salmon, and this is typically served with scrambled eggs and dill or mustard sauce. Then there are the many guises of pickled herring and anchovy, which adorn the main dinner table as well as being eaten for "aftons", a snack often taken later in the evening.

The ancient seafarers' staple of stockfish (also called tørrfisk or clipfish), the unsalted fish that is dried hard in the open air, is a highly nutritious ingredient used within various fish dishes. The distinctive taste of lutefisk, another long-established speciality, which is created with salted and dried cod soaked in a lye solution, produces a jelly-like substance which is eaten with boiled potatoes and flatbread, traditionally on Christmas Eve or at Easter.

Another classic Scandinavian fish dish is gravlaks, as it is known in Norway. This is made with oily fish smothered with salt, and then buried in the ground to preserve it. Left for under a week, the flesh cures to produce the clean flavour and smooth texture of gravlaks. If the fish is left longer, for up to several months, the flesh ferments into a sour product with an individual smell known as rakefisk, an acquired taste, which is usually served with raw red onion rings, boiled potatoes, butter, lefse (traditional bread) and sour cream.

Fruit and sweets

Many Norwegian desserts feature fruits and berries, which mature slowly in the cold climate, producing a smaller volume with a rich taste. Fruit soup, a speciality of Scandinavia, is made with seasonal fruits, often cooked with tapioca. Another traditional dessert is rødgrøt, a fruit pudding made from red fruit juices. Norwegians are also big coffee drinkers and an important social pastime is "kaffe", coffee served with kaffebrød (coffee bread), cakes or waffles with jam and cream in the afternoon or early evening.

Traditional foodstuffs

The wild expanses of Norway and its natural supplies of fish, game, dairy products, vegetables and fruit mean that fresh and preserved local foodstuffs form the basis of the cuisine. Ingredients such as Atlantic cod and salmon, wild meats such as elk (moose), and forest fruits such as the native lingonberry are constantly reinvented in dishes of the country. In common with other Scandinavian countries, ingredients are used simply and effectively to maximize their flavours.

Fish and shellfish

One of Norway's most important staple foods has always been fish. Cod is still a crucial mainstay of the diet and economy, and herring rivals cod in popularity. Other popular fish include sprat, haddock, mackerel, capelin, sandeel, ling, ocean perch, coalfish, blenny and catfish. Once-plentiful supplies have been depleted by over-fishing, however, making cod a luxury, and herring, once a cheap treat, quite expensive. Norwegian seas also offer shellfish: prawns, mussels and Norway lobsters, also known as Dublin Bay prawns or langoustine. Norway lobster is smaller and has a brighter, pinker shell than the American variety.

Norwegian salmon is regarded all over the world as of the highest quality. Salmo salar, Atlantic salmon, has long provided great fishing in its unpolluted waters and favourable Gulf Stream temperatures.

Norway's lakes and rivers also yield a rich harvest of fish, with perch, grayling, bream, arctic char, tench, eel, and, in the south, brown trout, inhabiting the clear and bright waters.

Domestic and wild meat

Beef is raised in the southern peninsula valleys and is a frequent sight on the Norwegian table. Sheep and goats are raised in the mountain and fjord areas. In summer, they are taken up to mountain pastures or out onto the islands. There they graze on the rich, green grass and develop meat with exceptional flavour. Lamb is very popular in Norway and forms the basis of many traditional dishes, such as the casserole fårikål.

The popular pastime of hunting has always provided Norwegians with valuable meat protein. Elk (moose) can be found throughout Norway, from the forests in the south right up to the lower part of Finnmark in the north. Norway also has large herds of both wild and domestic reindeer (caribou), as well as deer in the south.

Smaller game also proliferate. Hare (jack rabbit) is found throughout the country, mostly on mountain moors but sometimes in woodland areas, too. Mountain ptarmigan (small grouse) live on high and stony mountainsides, with larger wood ptarmigan in the forests. Black and wood grouse are considered at their most delicious in autumn, when they are plump after a plentiful summer of berries, a diet that helps to produce flavoursome flesh.

Below, left to right: Salted herring; fresh Atlantic cod; marinated herring, or sild, canned as sardines.

Vegetables

While the range is not large, vegetables grow well. Root vegetables such as turnips, parsnips, cabbage, carrots and swedes (rutabagas) that can be stored for winter are all favourites. Best loved of all is the potato. Not only is it used as a vegetable at almost every meal, potato flour thickens sauces and casseroles and is also mixed with wheat flour for lighter cakes. Cabbage is a much-used vegetable and Norway's pickled version of the German sauerkraut, surkål, is so popular that today various ready-prepared versions are bought in large quantities. Cauliflower and broccoli are also well liked.

Cereals and beans

The main cereals are barley, a grain tolerant of a wide range of soils and climates, oats and rye. Barley in particular was made into porridge, used whole in soups and stews, or ground to use as a flour. Though rich in protein and starch, barley contains no gluten. It is used to make the traditional Scandinavian flat bread, and is an important ingredient in many of the hardbreads Norway is so famous for. Dried peas, such as the Scandinavian yellow pea, provide a sustaining base for warming soups.

Cultivated fruits

Only three per cent of Norway is arable land and most of this is concentrated in the wooded valleys of the south. The area around Hardangerfjord, near Bergen, is the main fruit-growing area. Apples, plums, cherries, apricots and other orchard fruit flourish. The long winters mean a short growing season, although this is to a certain extent compensated for by the length of the days. Slow ripening in the temperate climate brings superlative flavour, while cool air means few insects.

Wild produce

The forests of Norway are home to a variety of wild fruit. In summer, there are wild strawberries and raspberries, which are intensely flavoured miniature versions of the cultivated varieties. Between mid-July and September a profusion of berries grow on low bushes: blueberries on open uplands; swamp-loving small bilberries; high-bush and low-bush cranberries; meskeg crowberries or lingonberries and the unparalleled cloudberries. These grow one per stalk and look slightly like an amber-colored, fat raspberry but have a unique flavour. Unlike most soft fruits, and because they have high benzoic acid content, they keep very

Above, left to right A selection of favourite Norwegian ingredients: raspberries, one of the region's many wild berries; cabbage, carrots and turnips, all staple vegetables; and pickled gherkins.

well. Cloudberries are notoriously difficult to find and considerable efforts are made by fruit pickers to protect their location.

In the woods are chanterelle and other wild mushrooms. Norwegians among many other Scandinavians, are keen mushroom gatherers and there are special checkpoints where the day's harvest can be checked for edibility.

Herbs and spices

Norwegians have not traditionally used many flavourings. Salt was always the most important seasoning but was used more as a preservative than an intensifier of flavour.

However, certain herbs and spices have become standards for adding flavour. Many, such as parsley, thyme and caraway, grow wild. Dill, closely associated with all Scandinavian food, particularly fish, is a member of the parsley family. The name comes from Old Norse, dilla, meaning "to lull" and dill water has long been used for soothing babies as a main ingredient in gripe water.

Juniper trees grow high in the mountains and their berries and young sprigs provide flavour, particularly with meat dishes but also as an alternative to dill for flavouring gravlaks. Birch twigs are a constant in Scandinavian cookery, used as whisks to produce lump-free sauces and stripped of their bark to give additional flavour to meat.

The two favourite Norwegian spices are cardamom and cinnamon. Cardamom, which comes mainly from India, is a favourite flavouring for a wide range of baked goods. Cinnamon is used in baking and in certain sweet dishes. Caraway is considered to be the oldest cultivated European spice plant. The Norwegians value it highly, especially for flavouring the cabbage dish surkål and certain casseroles. Peppercorns, too, play an important part. Norwegians appreciate that if whole peppercorns are cooked slowly in a casserole, their flavour is softened and transformed.

Dairy and cheese products
Norwegians have always valued dairy products and practically every small farm had at least one cow. When barter was common practice, butter was one of the most coveted items of currency. Historically, sour milk and cream were

an important part of the diet and they are still popular. The daily drink used to be blande, sour milk mixed with water, and this is still a favourite.

Norway has a rich cheese tradition. The smooth texture of most makes them easy to slice with a special flat-bladed cutter. This tool has an attractive rounded shape with a handle and pares off wafer-thin slices from any hard or semi-hard cheese.

A variety of cheese known as mysost is made from milk whey heated very slowly in immense copper pans over a wood fire, leaving a brown, caramelized paste called prim, which is then packed into moulds. These cheeses vary in colour from light to dark brown, are sweet to the taste but rather strong. As they dry out very quickly, the cheeses are sealed with paraffin wax before being stored. They are served in thin slices.

Gammelost is made mainly in western Norway, with the finest coming from the Hardanger and Sogn districts. Made with naturally soured cow's milk (which contains no rennet), and round and flat, it has a green-blue-brownish veining that traditionally came from naturally occurring fungus spores present in the farm's dairy. Today the fungus spores are artificially impregnated.

Above, left to right Cardamom pods are a favourite flavouring; juniper berries often accompany meat dishes; and ekte gjetost, the pure goat's milk cheese.

Most people associate Norway with Jarlsberg, a semi-hard cheese with the large holes and pale colour of Emmental, though it is slightly creamier in texture and nuttier in flavour. Other Norwegian cheeses include gräddost, a soft cheese used in open sandwiches; ridder, which has a piquant flavour that deepens with age and is at its sharpest when supplied in its distinctive orange outer coating; sveitser, with large holes and a rich, sweet, slightly nutty flavour like Jarlsberg; nøkkelost, which includes caraway and cloves, giving it a slightly acidic flavour; and geitost, a cheese that looks caramelized and is made from the whey of goat's milk.

Bread and baking
A favourite Norwegian cooking activity is baking and bread, whether fresh or hard, has always been a mainstay of the country's diet. In fact, there is a local word, pålegg, meaning "something to put on bread" – this could be something simple, a piece of cheese or ham, or a more complicated

arrangement for an open sandwich, which can use a base of wheat and rye bread or hardbread.

Hardbreads were prepared from the autumn grain harvest and were stored for consumption during the winter. Some hardbreads are round with a hole in the middle, enabling them to be threaded on sticks for easy storage. Others are rectangular in shape. They vary from very thin to much thicker.

Flat bread, or flatbrød, is made with barley flour, salt and water and is eaten with salted meats and soups. Another traditional bread, called lefse, was popular among fishermen because it would keep fresh during their trips. When dried out, lefse can be softened by being wrapped in a damp towel. There are many recipes, some with flour, some with potatoes. Lefse is usually eaten spread with softened butter and sprinkled with sugar.

The Norwegian enthusiasm for baking is apparent in the popularity of elaborate gateaux for dessert such as Bløtkake (cream layer cake), with various fruits, and Kvaefjord Cake with vanilla cream, meringue and almonds. Tilslørte Bondepiker (veiled country girls), is made with apples, cream and caramelized breadcrumbs. Yeast sweet breads are also popular and every Norwegian cook has a range of favourite biscuits or cookies, such

as Berlin Wreath Biscuits or Vanilla Christmas Biscuits. The spectacular Kransekake, made with almond rings, sometimes reaching a height of two feet, is seen as the national cake and is made to celebrate special occasions. Sometimes a bottle of wine is hidden inside, gradually revealed as the rings are eaten.

Drink

The most famous Scandinavian drink is akevitt or aquavit, seen as a cure for all ills. Norway's akevitt is now made from potatoes, and is flavoured with caraway seed. Modern distilleries often add flavour with orange, coriander (cilantro), anise or fennel, as well as sugar and salt. The spirit is aged from three to five years in oak barrels previously used for sherry. Exported to Australia, unsold barrels returned to Norway. As soon as producers realized these had developed a superior flavour, they marketed their akevitt as having crossed the line twice, once on the way to Australia and once on the way back. The traditional flask is divided into four or five stems, enabling the liquid to be thoroughly cooled. Some people like to bury the bottle in a block of ice to ensure the fiery liquid is completely chilled.

Beer chasers often accompany akevitt, and beer has been home-brewed in Norway for centuries. Beer is still the drink

Above, left to right Three of the most famous Norwegian products: Jarlsberg cheese; crispbread; and akevitt, often accompanied by a beer chaser.

of choice for many Norwegians and is produced in a variety of alcoholic levels, the higher ones controlled by the state. Aquavit and beer are the traditional accompaniments to such dishes such as lutefisk or fårikål.

Today, wine has taken over as a major alcoholic beverage, with consumption paralleling most west European countries. In 1919 Norwegians voted for prohibition. By 1927, when the ban ended, it was reckoned that half the population was either bootlegging or operating an illegal still. The state took charge of the sale and production of all alcohol except beer. It remained a state monopoly until 1990, when European law prohibited state monopolies for import and production. The sale of alcohol, though, is still strictly controlled through a special, state-run, chain of stores.

Norway also produces vodkas, bottled water and fruit juices. The only drink that rivals the popularity of akevitt is coffee, an integral part of Norwegian social life, enjoyed by 80 per cent of the population both before and after meals, with desserts and with spirits.

The cold table

Marinated salt herrings

Herrings with carrot and leek

Herrings with onion and tomato

Salted herrings in sherry

Marinated salmon

Crab salad with coriander

Bird's nest salad

Pickled beetroot

Baked ham omelette

Liver pâté

Herb-cured fillet of elk with sour
    cream sauce

A shared celebration

The Norwegian cold table, or koldt bord, has its roots in a time when food was scarce and there was often a considerable distance between friends and neighbours. When invited for a meal, each guest would bring a contribution – all the dishes were then placed on the table and everyone served themselves. This ensured that the costs of a meal were shared while still providing a good night's entertainment.

An essential component of a well-stocked koldt bord is pickled or salted herrings served with various sauces and flavourings. Fish might include a whole glazed trout or salmon, marinated fish such as gravlaks, and smoked fish. There are whole hams, roast cuts of meat and ready-cut cured meats, known as spekemat, made from salted, smoked, or marinated reindeer (caribou), mutton or lamb, as well as a wide variety of sausages and pâtés. These are accompanied by various salads, dishes such as pickled beetroot (beet) or cucumber and a selection of breads and hardbreads. There is also a cheeseboard, usually arranged with a selection of radishes, celery, and strips of sweet (bell) peppers, or alternatively with grapes or slices of ripe pear. A variety of desserts are offered, almost certainly including a glorious layer cake.

There is a strict etiquette to serving oneself. Starting with the cured herrings and other fish, guests take a little food on a small plate. They may go back for a second helping, even a third. Then, on a different plate, they can approach the meat dishes. It is understood that many trips can be made to the table so that dishes can be sampled individually. Plates should not be piled up with lots of different foods because each flavour needs to be appreciated on its own.

Marinated salt herrings
Spekesild

Marinated herrings are essential to the cold table. This basic marinade has many variations, one of the most delicious being when mixed with sour cream and chopped chives.

Serves 4 as an appetizer

2 salt herring fillets or 2 jars (150–200g/5–7oz) herring fillets in brine, drained (these do not need soaking)

200ml/7fl oz/scant 1 cup water

400ml/14fl oz/1⅔ cups wine vinegar

150g/5oz/¾ cup sugar

1 onion, sliced

1 bay leaf, 6 whole allspice and 6 whole peppercorns

fresh dill fronds and sliced onions, to garnish

1 Soak the herring fillets in cold water for 8–12 hours. Drain, rinse under cold water and place in a glass jar.

2 Put the water, vinegar and sugar in a large bowl and stir until the sugar has dissolved. Add the onion, bay leaf, allspice and peppercorns then pour over the herring fillets. Leave in a cold place for 6–12 hours before serving.

3 To serve, cut the fillets into 2.5cm/1in thick slices and arrange on a serving dish. Garnish with dill and sliced onions.

Per portion Energy 310kcal/1311kJ; Protein 12.9g; Carbohydrate 47.9g, of which sugars 47.5g; Fat 8.4g, of which saturates 0g; Cholesterol 32mg; Calcium 34mg; Fibre 0.2g; Sodium 625mg.

Herrings with carrot and leek
Spekesild med Gulrötter

Marinated herrings can be dressed in a number of different ways. Here, they are combined with the fresh taste of carrot and leek for a tasty appetizer.

Serves 4 as an appetizer

2 salt herring fillets or 2 jars (150–200g/5–7oz) herring fillets in brine, drained (these do not need soaking)

200ml/7fl oz/¾ cup water

400ml/14fl oz/1⅔ cups wine vinegar

150g/5oz/¾ cup sugar

1 small carrot, finely sliced

½ small leek, white part only, finely sliced

2 shallots, quartered

1 After soaking and marinating the herrings following steps 1 and 2 of the Marinated Salt Herrings, cut the herring fillets into 2.5cm/1in thick pieces then arrange the pieces on a serving dish as if they were still whole.

2 Add a little of the marinade to the fillets and then the sliced carrot and leek. Place the quartered shallots around the edge of the dish and serve.

Per portion Energy 174kcal/731kJ; Protein 13.2g; Carbohydrate 10.9g, of which sugars 10.3g; Fat 8.5g, of which saturates 0.1g; Cholesterol 32mg; Calcium 24mg; Fibre 1.2g; Sodium 628mg.

Herrings with onion and tomato
Spekesild med Lök og Tomat

This is another way of dressing the basic marinated herring recipe, using a classic combination with slices of onion and tomato that is always popular.

Serves 4 as an appetizer

2 salt herring fillets (prepared as in the recipe for Marinated Salt Herrings) or 2 jars (150–200g/5–7oz) herring fillets in brine, drained (these do not need soaking)

1 onion, finely sliced

1 large tomato, skinned and thinly sliced

fresh dill fronds, to garnish

1 After soaking and marinating the herrings following steps 1 and 2 of the Marinated Salt Herrings, cut the herring fillets into 2.5cm/1in thick pieces then arrange the pieces on a serving dish as if they were still whole.

2 Add a little of the marinade to the fillets and then arrange the onion and tomato slices, overlapping, on top. Serve garnished with dill fronds.

Cook's tip Accompany marinated herrings with thickly buttered dark rye bread and ice-cold snaps with beer chasers.

Per portion Energy 165kcal/694kJ; Protein 12.8g; Carbohydrate 9.3g, of which sugars 8.9g; Fat 8.4g, of which saturates 0g; Cholesterol 32mg; Calcium 15mg; Fibre 0.4g; Sodium 625mg.

Salted herrings in sherry
Sherrysild

This recipe uses matjes herrings rather than pre-marinated ones. Here, the marinade is formed of water, sherry, vinegar and sugar – easy to prepare and tasty to eat.

Serves 4 as an appetizer

2–3 matjes herrings

60ml/4 tbsp water

100ml/3½fl oz/scant ½ cup medium-dry sherry

30ml/2 tbsp wine vinegar

45ml/3 tbsp sugar

1 onion, finely sliced

5 peppercorns, crushed

fresh dill fronds, to garnish

1 The matjes herrings will not need marinating. Cut the herrings into 2.5cm/1in pieces and arrange on a serving dish. Put the water, sherry and vinegar in a jug (pitcher), add the sugar and stir until dissolved.

2 Pour the dressing over the herrings. Arrange the sliced onion on top and sprinkle with the crushed peppercorns. Leave to marinate in a cold place for 2–3 hours. Serve garnished with dill fronds.

Per portion Energy 228kcal/960kJ; Protein 12.8g; Carbohydrate 20.7g, of which sugars 20.4g; Fat 8.4g, of which saturates 0g; Cholesterol 32mg; Calcium 21mg; Fibre 0.2g; Sodium 626mg.

Marinated salmon
Gravlaks

It was the Swedes who first made salmon marinated with dill popular, but Norway, with its plentiful supply of salmon, wasn't far behind. Norwegians marinate the fish with dill but also use juniper sprigs as an alternative and, although the traditional marinade has equal quantities of salt and sugar, modern tastes often prefer a little more sugar to salt. Trout, herring and mackerel can be marinated in the same way as salmon.

1 Scrape the scales off the fish. Leave the skin on as it makes the fish much easier to slice after marinating. Wipe the fish with damp kitchen paper.

2 Mix together the salt, sugar and the peppercorns. Using a shallow dish, close to the size of the fish, line with a piece of foil large enough to wrap the fish in, and a layer of juniper or dill. Place one piece of fish, skin side down, on the juniper or dill. Rub one third of the salt mixture into the flesh and add a layer of juniper or dill. Rub another third of the salt into the flesh of the second piece of fish and place on the first, matching thinner side to thicker so that the fish makes as even a parcel as possible. Rub the last third of salt mixture into the top skin and add the remaining juniper or dill.

3 Sprinkle the Cognac over the fish. Cover with the foil, place a small board on top and weight the fish down. Leave in cool pantry or refrigerator for 36–48 hours, depending on the thickness of the fish.

4 For the sauce, use all ingredients at room temperature. Mix the egg yolk, mustard and sugar together and drizzle the oil into the mixture, whisking to form a thick, shiny sauce. Whisk in the vinegar and add the juniper or dill and season.

5 Scrape all the seasonings off the marinated fish and remove any bones. Slice the fish (thick slices are traditional), from one end, at 45 degrees. Serve garnished with lemon wedges and dill and accompany with the mustard sauce.

Per portion Energy 479kcal/1981kJ; Protein 26.3g; Carbohydrate 0.4g, of which sugars 0.3g; Fat 40.4g, of which saturates 6.4g; Cholesterol 113mg; Calcium 35mg; Fibre 0g; Sodium 169mg.

Serves 3–4

500g/1¼lb middle cut of salmon, or fat trout, mackerel or herring fillets, with skin on

25g/1oz/2 tbsp crushed sea salt

25–50g/1–2oz/2–4 tbsp sugar

5ml/1 tsp crushed white peppercorns

15ml/1 tbsp chopped fresh juniper sprigs or dill, plus extra to garnish

15ml/1 tbsp Cognac

lemon wedges, to garnish

For the mustard sauce

1 egg yolk

15ml/1 tbsp sweet Scandinavian mustard

15ml/1 tbsp sugar

150ml/¼ pint/⅔ cup light olive oil

15ml/1 tbsp white wine vinegar

15–30ml/1–2 tbsp chopped juniper sprigs or 30–45ml/2–3 tbsp chopped fresh dill

salt and ground black pepper

Cook's tip This sauce can be made without the egg yolk but this makes it more liable to separate. Dried dill can be used to replace the fresh dill but in this case allow the sauce to stand for several hours to allow the flavour to develop.

Serves 4 as an appetizer, 2 as a light meal

1 head romaine lettuce

2 eating apples

juice 1 lemon

1 bunch spring onions (scallions), chopped

150ml/¼ pint/⅔ cup whipping cream

135ml/4½fl oz crème fraîche

30ml/2 tbsp chopped fresh coriander (cilantro), plus extra to garnish

brown and white meat of 2 crabs

salt

Crab salad with coriander
Krabbesalat med koriander

Crab, like other shellfish from the North Sea around Norway, is full of flavour. Norwegians love crab when it is simply dressed and accompanied with chopped hard-boiled eggs or served in a mixed salad, such as this one. The crab's richness is blended with two types of cream, contrasting with the freshness of the apples and spring onions. Coriander gives an extra punch to the flavour.

1 Shred the lettuce and arrange around the edge of a shallow serving bowl. Peel, quarter and core the apples then cut into small dice. Put in a bowl, add the lemon juice and toss together. Add the spring onions and mix together.

2 Whisk the cream in a large bowl until it stands in soft peaks, then fold in the crème fraîche. Add the apple mixture and chopped coriander.

3 Mix together the brown and white crab meat and season with salt to taste. Fold the meat into the cream mixture. Check the seasoning and put in the centre of the lettuce. Serve garnished with chopped coriander.

Per portion Energy 382kcal/1585kJ; Protein 20.6g; Carbohydrate 6.4g, of which sugars 6.2g; Fat 30.6g, of which saturates 19.3g; Cholesterol 151mg; Calcium 188mg; Fibre 1.4g; Sodium 571mg.

Bird's nest salad
Fuglerede

This is a particularly attractive dish on the cold table. The ingredients are arranged, as the name suggests, in the shape of a bird's nest encircling a raw egg yolk. All the ingredients, including the yolk, should be stirred together by the first person to help themselves to the dish.

1 Using a medium, round serving dish, place two egg cups in it, upside down. In successive circles around the cups, arrange the anchovies, capers and potatoes. Add the beetroot and onions around the edge of the dish.

2 Carefully remove the egg cups. Break the eggs, one at a time, separating the yolks from the whites, and carefully put the whole egg yolks where the egg cups were positioned. Alternatively, use egg shell halves to hold the yolks.

Per portion Energy 93kcal/390kJ; Protein 5.9g; Carbohydrate 10.1g, of which sugars 2.3g; Fat 3.6g, of which saturates 0.9g; Cholesterol 99mg; Calcium 41mg; Fibre 0.9g; Sodium 284mg.

Serves 4

8 anchovy fillets, roughly chopped

30ml/2 tbsp capers

2 potatoes, cooked, cooled and diced, total quantity 45ml/3 tbsp

45ml/3 tbsp chopped pickled beetroot (beet)

15–30ml/1–2 tbsp finely diced onion

2 very fresh eggs

Cook's tip Raw egg yolk should not be served to children, the elderly, pregnant women, convalescents or anyone suffering from an illness. The eggs must be very fresh.

Pickled beetroot
Syltede Rødbeter

Lightly pickled, these sweet-sour beetroots accompany a wide variety of foods throughout Scandinavia and almost always appear on the Norwegian cold table. The beetroot should be left to marinate after it has been prepared and you can keep it in the refrigerator for up to three weeks.

1 Put the sliced beetroot into sterilized jars if storing the beetroot or in a bowl if eating soon after it has been prepared. Put the vinegar, water, sugar, salt and pepper in a stainless-steel or enamel pan, bring to the boil then reduce the heat and simmer for 2 minutes.

2 Pour the hot marinade over the beetroot and add the cloves or caraway seeds, if using. Seal the jars or cover the bowl and leave the beetroot to marinate for at least 24 hours or preferably 2–3 days before serving. Serve after it has marinated or store in the refrigerator for up to 3 weeks.

Per portion Energy 73kcal/310kJ; Protein 0.7g; Carbohydrate 18.5g, of which sugars 18.3g; Fat 0g, of which saturates 0g; Cholesterol 0mg; Calcium 16mg; Fibre 0.7g; Sodium 353mg.

Serves 4–6

about 225g/8oz cooked, small beetroot (beet), skinned and thinly sliced

150ml/¼ pint/²⁄₃ cup white wine vinegar

150ml/¼ pint/²⁄₃ cup water

90g/3½oz/½ cup sugar

5ml/1 tsp salt

4–5 cloves or 5ml/1 tsp caraway seeds (optional)

ground black pepper

Cook's tip A small piece of horseradish added to each jar helps to prevent mould from forming.

Serves 4

15g/¹⁄₂oz/1 tbsp butter, plus extra
for greasing

1 leek, white and pale green parts only,
thinly sliced, or 1 shallot, chopped

4 eggs

300ml/¹⁄₂ pint/1¹⁄₄ cups single
(light) cream

115g/4oz cooked ham, preferably
smoked, diced

salt and ground black pepper

chopped fresh parsley, to garnish

Cook's tip Cooked chicken or
smoked sausage can be used as an
alternative to the cooked ham, and
the omelette can be topped with
grated cheese.

Baked ham omelette
Ovnsomelett

The Norwegians have a gift for turning leftovers into something special, as illustrated by this baked omelette. It is equally good served hot or cold. Cut into small squares, it can be served with drinks, or it can be placed on a cold table. With a salad it provides a light lunch or supper dish. In Norway it might be served as one of the "aftons" or snacks that are produced in the late evening to compensate for the main meal of the day being served so early.

1 Preheat the oven to 180°C/350°F/Gas 4. Butter an ovenproof dish measuring about 20cm/8in in diameter. Melt the butter in a pan, add the leek or shallot and fry for 2–3 minutes. Break the eggs into a bowl and beat lightly together. Add the cream, season with salt and pepper and beat together until well combined. Add the chopped ham.

2 Pour the mixture into the prepared dish and bake in the oven for about 25 minutes, until set and golden brown. Serve immediately, garnished with chopped parsley.

Per portion Energy 287kcal/1190kJ; Protein 14.8g; Carbohydrate 3.2g, of which sugars 2.9g; Fat 24.1g, of which saturates 13g; Cholesterol 256mg; Calcium 109mg; Fibre 1g; Sodium 460mg.

Serves 6–8

butter, for greasing

250g/9oz hard back pork fat, thinly sliced

500g/1¼lb pig's liver

1 onion, chopped

5 anchovy fillets

60ml/4 tbsp plain (all-purpose) flour

100ml/3½fl oz/scant ½ cup milk

100ml/3½fl oz/scant ½ cup double (heavy) cream

2 large eggs

1.5ml/¼ tsp ground cloves

1.5ml/¼ tsp ground allspice

pinch of cayenne pepper

115g/4oz/1⅔ cup mushrooms, chopped and sautéed in butter (optional)

salt and ground black pepper

Cook's tip The pâté's smoothness depends upon the fine mincing or processing of the liver and the other ingredients.
Variation Cook slices of apple in a little butter until translucent, sprinkle them with sugar and cook until almost caramelized. Use to garnish the pâté.

Liver pâté
Leverpostei

Traditionally, every Norwegian cook had their favourite pâté recipe. The majority are made with pig's liver, as in this recipe, which is simple to prepare, and best eaten a couple of days after cooking to allow its flavours to develop fully.

1 Preheat the oven to 180°C/350°F/Gas 4. Generously butter a 1kg/2¼lb loaf tin (pan). Line the bottom of the tin, using about a third of the sliced pork fat.

2 Cut the pig's liver and the remaining pork fat into small pieces and mince (grind) with the onion and anchovy fillets. For the best results, the mixture should be put through a mincer (grinder) at least three times and five is better. Alternatively, use a blender or food processor to mince the ingredients together. If using a blender or food processor, then push the mixture through a sieve (strainer) after mincing because these machines tend to leave odd strings of membrane. This process sounds hard work, but it does ensure a really smooth pâté. Only mincing once or using a blender or processor without sieving will produce a coarser result but the flavour should still be excellent.

3 Add the flour, milk, cream, eggs, cloves, allspice, cayenne pepper and mushrooms, if using, to the mixture and season with salt and pepper. Mix well together and pour into the prepared loaf tin.

4 Cover the loaf tin with buttered foil, place in a roasting pan and fill with hot water to come about two-thirds of the way up the sides of the pan. Bake in the oven for about 1 hour, until the tip of a sharp knife, inserted in the centre, comes out clean. Leave the pâté to cool in the tin before serving.

Per portion Energy 588kcal/2433kJ; Protein 21.4g; Carbohydrate 1.85g, of which sugars 1.6g; Fat 55.2g, of which saturates 23.9g; Cholesterol 344mg; Calcium 52mg; Fibre 0.1g; Sodium 202mg.

Serves 8–10 as an appetizer, 4 as a main course

30ml/2 tbsp salt

60ml/4 tbsp sugar

90ml/6 tbsp chopped mixed fresh herbs, such as basil, marjoram, thyme, parsley, rosemary and juniper sprigs

100ml/3½fl oz/scant ½ cup red wine

60ml/4 tbsp virgin olive oil

500g/1¼lb fillet of elk or red or fallow deer (or alternatively venison or beef)

ground black pepper

For the sour cream sauce

150g/5oz cranberry jam, or lingonberry jam or berries

135ml/4½fl oz sour cream

15–30ml/1–2 tbsp sugar (if fresh berries are being used)

Cook's tips

• If the meat is partially frozen after it has been marinated, it is easier to slice thinly.

• Juniper sprigs are the new shoots at the end of branches. You can use 2–3 crushed juniper berries instead – the flavour will be slightly different, but still delicious.

Herb-cured fillet of elk with sour cream sauce
Urtemarinert dyrestek med rømmesaus

The roots of this recipe can be found in the traditional practice of finding ways of preserving food in a population that had to be self-sufficient through the long winters. This herb-cured fillet of elk can be seen as a game equivalent of marinated salmon. Nowadays there is no need to marinate meat, but the method continues because of its delicious flavour. In traditional recipes, elk or red deer are used, but the same method can be applied to fillet of venison or beef.

1 Put the salt, sugar, chopped herbs, wine and olive oil in a bowl. Season generously with pepper and then stir together until well mixed.

2 Put the meat in a strong plastic bag, add the marinade and ensure that it covers the meat. Place the bag in the refrigerator and leave the meat to marinate for 3 days, turning over the bag at least twice a day.

3 To make the sour cream sauce with cranberry or lingonberry jam, put the jam in a bowl, add the sour cream and mix well together. If using fresh cranberries or lingonberries, put them in a bowl, add sugar to taste, crush together with a fork, and stir in the sour cream, mixing well.

4 To serve, slice the meat very thinly and accompany with the sour cream sauce. To serve the fillet as a main course, accompany with roast vegetables and boiled potatoes.

Per portion Energy 187kcal/780kJ; Protein 11.3g; Carbohydrate 11.1g, of which sugars 11.1g; Fat 10.4g, of which saturates 3.8g; Cholesterol 39mg; Calcium 29mg; Fibre 0.3g; Sodium 37mg.

Soups

Nutrition and warmth

The word "soup" can be applied to a vast range of dishes, from a clear broth or consommé to a thick, hearty concoction containing larger pieces of meat or fish that is almost a stew.

Especially in rural Norway, soup has always been a key way to provide a nutritious meal. Because early wooden houses seldom had an oven, cooking was done in a pot, either on a stove that may have been the only source of heat in the home, or over an open fire. Even now, while soup is often the starting point of a meal before moving on to a more substantial main course, it also forms a meal in itself, particularly when accompanied with hardbread or a roll plus cheese. Norwegians usually lunch lightly and, though a sandwich of some sort is common, on cold winter days a bowl of hot soup can be most welcome.

As might be expected in a nation that eats fish regularly, fish soup is a perennial favourite, inspired by whatever local fish is available. For meat soups, Norwegians often make two dishes out of one cooking process, using the poaching liquid as a soup and the meat that has been gently cooking in the pot sliced as a separate course. The Sami, descendants of the earliest Norwegian settlers and herders of reindeer (caribou), make a soup with reindeer flesh, which is so substantial it could be classed as a stew. Then there are vegetable soups, many containing the favourite ingredients of mushrooms and dried yellow peas. And not all soups are savoury – throughout Scandinavia, fruit is often used to make delicious versions, such as the juniper and apple one that appears here.

Wild mushroom soup
Soppsuppe

A large proportion of Norway is forested and wild mushrooms are plentiful. Norwegians are skilled at knowing which ones are edible and which ones should be avoided. Late summer and autumn are the best times to go mushroom hunting. One way of using the harvest is in this soup.

1 If using dried mushrooms, put in a small bowl and pour over a generous amount of boiling water. Leave to soak for at least 20 minutes, until the mushrooms are soft. Using a slotted spoon, remove the mushrooms from the bowl then strain the soaking liquid and reserve. Chop the dried mushrooms.

2 Put the sliced mushrooms in a pan, cover with the stock and simmer for 10 minutes. Strain the stock and reserve.

3 Melt the butter in a large pan, add the sliced mushrooms and the soaked mushrooms and fry gently for 2–3 minutes, then season with salt and pepper.

4 Stir the flour into the pan and cook over a low heat for 1–2 minutes, without colouring. Remove from the heat and gradually stir in the reserved stock and the dried mushroom soaking liquid to form a smooth sauce. Return to the heat and, stirring all the time, cook until the sauce boils and thickens. Lower the heat and simmer gently for 5–10 minutes.

5 Add the cream to the soup then add lemon juice to taste. Finally, add the sherry, if using. Pour the soup into individual serving bowls and top with a little cream swirled on top of each and a final garnish of chopped parsley.

Per portion Energy 154kcal/638kJ; Protein 3.2g; Carbohydrate 9.3g, of which sugars 0.5g; Fat 11.8g, of which saturates 7.2g; Cholesterol 29mg; Calcium 26mg; Fibre 1.6g; Sodium 82mg.

Serves 4

10g/¹⁄₄oz/1 tbsp dried mushrooms, such as ceps, if wild mushrooms are unavailable

400g/14oz mushrooms, preferably wild, sliced

1.25 litres/2¹⁄₄ pints/5¹⁄₂ cups light stock, vegetable or chicken

50g/2oz/4 tbsp butter

30–45ml/2–3 tbsp plain (all-purpose) white flour

60ml/4 tbsp double (heavy) cream, plus extra to garnish

a squeeze of fresh lemon juice

15–30ml/1–2 tbsp medium sherry (optional)

salt and ground black pepper

chopped fresh parsley, to garnish

Cook's tips

• Wild mushrooms have a deep, meaty flavour which gives a rich tang to this soup.

• Choose mushrooms to suit your taste, either combining varieties or focusing on a single one such as chanterelle or cep.

Serves 4

15ml/1 tbsp juniper berries

4 cardamom pods

3 whole allspice

1 small cinnamon stick

bunch of fresh parsley

30ml/2 tbsp olive oil

3 cooking apples, peeled, cored and diced

2 celery sticks, finely chopped

2 shallots, chopped

2.5cm/1in piece fresh root ginger, finely chopped

1 litre/1¾ pints/4 cups light chicken stock

250ml/8fl oz/1 cup cider

250ml/8fl oz/1 cup double (heavy) cream

75ml/5 tbsp Armagnac (optional)

salt and ground black pepper

chopped fresh parsley, to garnish

Juniper and apple soup
Eplesuppe med enerbær

This is an example of the savoury fruit soups that are popular throughout northern Europe. The apple and juniper flavours are particularly Norwegian. Here it's the berries that are being used, not the fresh young shoots.

1 Put the juniper berries, cardamom pods, allspice and cinnamon stick in a piece of muslin (cheesecloth) and tie together with string. Tie the parsley together.

2 Heat the oil in a pan, add the apples, celery, shallots and ginger, and season with salt and pepper. Place a piece of dampened baking parchment on top, cover the pan and cook gently for 10 minutes. Discard the parchment.

3 Add the stock and cider and stir well. Add the spices and parsley. Bring slowly to the boil, then lower the heat and simmer for 40 minutes. Remove the spices and parsley.

4 Pour the soup into a blender and blend until smooth. Then pass it through a sieve (strainer) into a clean pan. Bring to the boil and add the cream and Armagnac, if using. Add salt and pepper if necessary. Serve hot, garnished with parsley.

Per portion Energy 406kcal/1677kJ; Protein 1.4g; Carbohydrate 8.5g, of which sugars 8.1g; Fat 39.2g, of which saturates 21.7g; Cholesterol 86mg; Calcium 48mg; Fibre 1.2g; Sodium 29mg.

Curry soup
Karrisuppe

Indian spices have been enjoyed in Norway for many centuries, particularly in the south of the country, and curry powder has enlivened many dishes. More recently, South-east Asian food has become popular and the coconut milk in this recipe replaces the more familiar cream.

1 Melt the butter in a pan, add the shallots and cook gently for about 5 minutes until softened but not coloured. Add the apple, season with salt and pepper and cook for another 2 minutes, until the apple is slightly softened.

2 Stir the curry paste and flour into the pan and cook over a low heat for 1–2 minutes, without colouring. Remove from the heat and gradually stir in the stock to form a smooth sauce. Return to the heat and, stirring all the time, cook until the sauce boils and thickens. Lower the heat and simmer gently for 10 minutes.

3 Add the coconut milk to the soup and stir well. Check the seasonings, adding salt and pepper if necessary. Pour the soup into individual serving bowls and serve with a swirl of cream or coconut milk on top of each and chopped parsley, to garnish.

Per portion Energy 195kcal/812kJ; Protein 1.7g; Carbohydrate 14.3g, of which sugars 7.6g; Fat 15g, of which saturates 9.2g; Cholesterol 37mg; Calcium 66mg; Fibre 1.3g; Sodium 200mg.

Serves 4

50g/2oz/4 tbsp butter

2 shallots, finely chopped

1 cooking apple, peeled, cored and chopped

10ml/2 tsp curry paste

30ml/2 tbsp plain (all-purpose) flour

1.25 litres/2¼ pints/5½ cups chicken or beef stock

400ml/14fl oz can unsweetened coconut milk

salt and ground black pepper

To garnish

60ml/4 tbsp double (heavy) cream or 4 tbsp of the coconut milk

chopped fresh parsley

Cook's tip For a smooth soup, blend the soup in a blender or food processor before reheating and serving.

Lobster and tomato soup
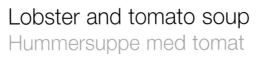
Hummersuppe med tomat

This luxurious lobster soup is for special occasions. The Norwegian lobster is smaller than those caught in the US, but its flesh is just as delicious. The soup can also be made with prawns, if you are feeling less extravagant, and is equally good. It is important to keep the shells as well as the flesh because they are used to provide additional flavour to the soup.

Serves 4

1 large cooked lobster or 500g/1¼lb/ 3 cups cooked prawns (shrimp)

25g/1oz/2 tbsp butter

30ml/2 tbsp finely chopped shallot

2 red (bell) peppers, seeded and chopped

2.5cm/1in root ginger, finely chopped

1 clove garlic, finely chopped

60ml/4 tbsp brandy

30ml/2 tbsp tomato purée (paste)

1.25 litres/2¼ pints/5½ cups water

15ml/1 tbsp sherry vinegar

15ml/1 tbsp sugar

4 ripe tomatoes, skinned, seeded and chopped, or 400g/14oz can tomatoes

juice of 1 lime

salt and ground black pepper

chopped fresh dill, to garnish

1 Remove the lobster or prawn meat from their shells, reserving the shells. Set the meat aside. Melt the butter in a pan, add the shallots, peppers, ginger and garlic and cook for 5 minutes. Add the shells and cook gently for a further 10 minutes.

2 Add the brandy to the pan and set alight. Stir in the tomato purée. Add the water, season lightly with salt and pepper, and bring slowly to the boil. Lower the heat and simmer very gently for 40 minutes.

3 Strain the mixture into a clean pan. Add the vinegar, sugar, tomatoes and lime juice to taste, and check the seasonings, adding salt and pepper only if necessary.

4 Divide the lobster or prawn meat between four individual serving bowls. Bring the soup to the boil then pour over the shellfish. Serve garnished with chopped dill.

Per portion Energy 275kcal/1155kJ; Protein 29.6g; Carbohydrate 14.1g, of which sugars 13.5g; Fat 7.8g, of which saturates 3.7g; Cholesterol 151mg; Calcium 99mg; Fibre 2.6g; Sodium 479mg.

Serves 4

25–40g/1–1½oz/2–3 tbsp butter plus 15g/½oz/1 tbsp for frying the mushrooms (see below)

450g/1lb reindeer or venison, finely diced

1 onion, chopped

3 potatoes, diced

3 carrots, diced

6 juniper berries, crushed

115g/4oz/1⅔ cups mushrooms, diced

60ml/4 tbsp sour cream, to garnish

salt and ground black pepper

Cook's tip Cooking the mushrooms separately, instead of adding them with the onion, produces a fresher result in the finished soup.

Reindeer soup
Bidos

This is called a soup but many would class it as a stew. It comes from the Sami people, the Laplanders, who have lived in the far north of Scandinavia for over a thousand years. Their economy is centred around reindeer, which provides the basis for this recipe. Whether a soup or a stew, this is a hearty dish.

1 Heat 25g/1oz/2 tbsp butter in a flameproof casserole dish, add the meat and fry until browned on all sides, adding a little extra butter if necessary. Transfer the meat to a plate. Add the onion to the dish and fry gently for about 5 minutes until softened. Add a little water to the dish, stirring to lift any sediment on the bottom of the dish.

2 Return the meat to the dish. Add the potatoes, carrots, juniper berries, 5ml/1 tsp salt, pepper and water to cover the meat. Bring to the boil then lower the heat and simmer for 15 minutes until the meat is tender.

3 Meanwhile, heat 15g/½ oz/1 tbsp butter in a pan, add the mushrooms and sauté until softened, then add to the soup and simmer for another 5 minutes.

4 Ladle the soup into individual serving bowls and serve hot, with a swirl of sour cream on top of each.

Per portion Energy 289kcal/1214kJ; Protein 27.6g; Carbohydrate 15.5g, of which sugars 3.9g; Fat 14.1g, of which saturates 8.1g; Cholesterol 87mg; Calcium 36mg; Fibre 1.7g; Sodium 144mg.

Meldal soup
Meldalssodd

This is a dish that is both a soup and a main course. It is the Norwegian equivalent of the French pot-au-feu, which is meat poached in a broth that is served as a soup, with the meat sliced and served as a main course.

1 Put the three pieces of meat in a large pan. Add the water, salt, peppercorns, ginger and bay leaf and bring to simmering point. Simmer gently for 1–1½ hours until the pieces of meat are tender.

2 Make the meatballs by rolling the sausage meat into small balls and set aside. To make the flour dumplings, put the cream and sugar in a pan and bring to the boil. Immediately add the flour and beat well with a wooden spoon until the mixture comes away smoothly from the sides of the pan. Remove from the heat and add the eggs, one at a time, beating well together until incorporated.

3 Season the dumplings with the nutmeg and salt. Wet your hands and roll the mixture into 16–20 small balls (best done when the dumplings can be put straight into the soup, otherwise place them on baking parchment or a wet plate).

4 When cooked, remove the meat and leave to cool. Slice, arrange on a serving dish, add a little cooking liquid to prevent the slices from drying out and cover the dish.

5 Skim the stock of any fat, add the onion, carrots, turnip or swede and cabbage. Bring to the boil then lower the heat and simmer for about 10 minutes until the vegetables are just tender.

6 Add the meatballs to the stock and continue simmering for 5 minutes. Add the dumplings to the stock and simmer for a further 5 minutes.

7 Ladle the soup, meatballs and dumplings into individual serving bowls and serve hot. Serve the sliced meat as a main course, accompanied by boiled potatoes.

Serves 8–10

500g/1¼lb boneless beef, such as brisket

500g/1¼lb boneless pork, such as leg or lean belly

500g/1¼lb boneless mutton or lamb, such as shoulder

3 litres/5 pints/12½ cups water

20ml/4 tsp salt

5ml/1 tsp peppercorns

2.5cm/1n piece fresh root ginger

1 bay leaf

250g/9oz sausage meat (bulk sausage)

15ml/1 tbsp chopped onion

4 carrots, cut into strips

1 turnip or swede (rutabaga), diced

½ small white cabbage, cut into small pieces

boiled potatoes, to serve

For the flour dumplings

200ml/7fl oz/scant 1 cup single (light) cream

25ml/1½ tbsp sugar

130g/4½oz plain (all-purpose) flour

2 eggs

pinch of grated nutmeg

pinch of salt

Per portion Energy 453kcal/1892kJ; Protein 38.4g; Carbohydrate 22.9g, of which sugars 10.2g; Fat 23.7g, of which saturates 10.5g; Cholesterol 158mg; Calcium 111mg; Fibre 2.9g; Sodium 351mg.

Fish & shellfish

Salt cod, stuffed salmon and creamed shellfish

Norway's long coast is scattered with fjords, and inland the rivers and lakes thread the mountains and valleys with bright, pollution-free waters that teem with freshwater fish. For many centuries the major part of the Norwegian economy was oriented around fish, and it was the staple food of the population. No wonder, then, that so many of the traditional dishes are fish based.

The Vikings travelled on dried cod, or stockfish. In the 19th century the Norwegians perfected the art of salting cod, known as klipfish, and this was adopted by the Portuguese and Spanish markets. When the Norwegians imported olive oil and tomatoes in this period, they began to appreciate new dishes that could be made from salted cod, such as the Spanish and Portuguese-inspired dishes, bacalao and bacalhau. Gravlaks, thin slices of salmon cured in salt, sugar and dill, is now a popular dish throughout the western world. While the recipe itself is credited to the Swedes, it was the Norwegians who first started burying oily fish to preserve it, "grav" meaning "hole in the ground" and "laks" meaning "salmon".

Norwegians particularly love fresh fish – large fish markets typically have tanks that keep the fish alive until it is sold. Fish is often cooked very simply. Cutlets might be poached and served, perhaps, with a butter sauce. Fillets of herring and mackerel are fried in butter with little more than a fine coating of flour.

More elaborate fish dishes include Salmon Rolls with Asparagus and Butter Sauce or Roasted Salmon with Honey and Mustard. Shellfish is a frequent feature of Norwegian cooking and crabs or prawns can be included in salads for the koldt bord. Prawns (shrimp) can be used to stuff salmon parcels or creamed to form the centrepiece of a spinach ring.

Roasted salmon with honey and mustard

Ovnsstekt laks med honing og sennep

The clear, unpolluted Norwegian fjords produce salmon of the highest quality. Norwegian salmon has an international reputation and is exported all over the world. Chefs everywhere like to experiment with new ways of presenting this delicious fish. The honey and mustard marinade in the following recipe is based on a marinade by Andreas Viestad, one of Norway's best-known food writers.

1 To make the marinade, put the oil, honey, mustard and lemon rind in a small bowl and mix together. Season the marinade with salt and pepper to taste.

2 Put the salmon fillets in an ovenproof dish or on a baking sheet lined with baking parchment and spread the marinade over the each fillet. Leave to marinate for 30 minutes.

3 Preheat the oven to 200°C/400°F/Gas 6. Roast the fish in the oven for 10–12 minutes, until the flesh flakes easily. Serve hot.

Per portion Energy 296kcal/1231kJ; Protein 25.9g; Carbohydrate 3.2g, of which sugars 3.2g; Fat 20g, of which saturates 3.2g; Cholesterol 63mg; Calcium 36mg; Fibre 0.4g; Sodium 178mg.

Serves 4

30ml/2 tbsp olive oil

15ml/1 tbsp honey

30ml/2 tbsp wholegrain French mustard

grated rind ½ lemon

4 salmon fillets, each about 150g/5oz

salt and ground black pepper

Serves 4

4 salmon steaks, each about 175g/6oz

about 1 litre/1¾ pints/4 cups water

45ml/3 tbsp salt

5ml/1 tsp whole peppercorns

1 lemon slice

1 onion slice

For the Sandefjord butter

100ml/3½ fl oz/scant ½ cup double (heavy) cream

225g/8oz/1 cup chilled unsalted butter, cut into small cubes

30–45ml/2–3 tbsp chopped fresh parsley or chives

To serve

boiled potatoes ·

cucumber salad

Variations

• The dish can also be prepared with trout steaks but you will need eight trout steaks, instead of four salmon steaks, to serve four people.

• Sandefjord butter can also be served with fillets of salmon that have been brushed with olive oil, seasoned, and roasted in an oven heated to 200°C/400°F/Gas 6 for 10–12 minutes, according to their thickness.

Poached salmon steaks with Sandefjord butter
Kokt laks med sandefjordsmør

For sheer simplicity raised to a high standard, this dish takes a lot of beating. Sandefjord butter is named after a town near the mouth of the Oslofjord. A shipping centre since the 14th century, it is now a seaside resort. The "butter" is actually a classic butter sauce and is the traditional Norwegian accompaniment to many fish dishes.

1 Put the fish steaks, in a single layer, in a pan and add the water to cover the steaks. If there is not enough water, add a little more. Add the salt, peppercorns, lemon and onion slice. Bring to the boil then lower the heat to below simmering point. (The water should just throw up the occasional bubble.) Poach the fish for 6–8 minutes, until the flesh easily loosens from the backbone.

2 To make the Sandefjord butter, pour the cream into a pan and slowly bring to the boil. Lower the heat and add the butter, in small pieces, whisking all the time until well incorporated before adding another piece. Do not allow the sauce to boil or it will separate. If you wish, the sauce can be kept warm by putting it in a bowl standing over a pan of gently simmering water.

3 Just before serving, add the parsley or chives to the sauce. Serve the fish with boiled potatoes and a cucumber salad, accompanied with the Sandefjord butter.

Per portion Energy 771kcal/3184kJ; Protein 26.3g; Carbohydrate 1.1g, of which sugars 1g; Fat 73.6g, of which saturates 40g; Cholesterol 217mg; Calcium 71mg; Fibre 0.6g; Sodium 406mg.

Salmon rolls with asparagus and butter sauce
Lakserulader med asparges

Asparagus has been a popular ingredient in Norway for many years and its green spears appear each year as a welcome sign of spring. The green contrasts beautifully with the pink flesh of the salmon in this recipe and each has a sweetness of flavour that marries perfectly.

Serves 4

4 thick or 8 thin asparagus spears

4 very thin slices salmon fillet, each weighing about 115g/4oz

juice 1 lemon

1 bunch fresh parsley, chopped, to serve

salt and ground black pepper

For the butter sauce

1 shallot, finely chopped

6 peppercorns

120ml/4fl oz/½ cup dry white wine

60ml/4 tbsp double (heavy) cream

200g/7oz/scant 1 cup butter, cut into small cubes

salt and ground black pepper

Cook's tip If you can't get the salmon sliced, buy a piece weighing around 600g/1⅓lb cut from the thick end of the fillet. Use a sharp, thin knife to cut across the salmon, slanting slightly down, as though slicing smoked salmon but rather more thickly. Any leftover pieces can be briefly steamed and added to a salad

1 Steam the asparagus spears for 6–8 minutes, according to their size, until tender. Refresh under cold running water, drain and set aside.

2 The slices of salmon should be wide enough to roll around the asparagus. Don't worry if they have to be patched together. Place the slices on a surface, season with salt and pepper, lay one or two asparagus spears across each slice and then roll the salmon around them. Place the rolls on a rack over a pan of boiling water, sprinkle with lemon juice, and cover and steam for 3–4 minutes until tender.

3 To make the butter sauce, put the shallot, peppercorns and wine in a small pan and heat gently until the wine has reduced to a tablespoonful. Strain and return to the pan. Add the cream, bring to the boil, and then lower the heat.

4 Add the butter to the sauce in small pieces, whisking all the time until well incorporated before adding another piece. Do not allow the sauce to boil or it will separate. Season the sauce with salt and pepper to taste, if necessary. If you wish, the sauce can be kept warm by putting it in a bowl, standing over a pan of gently simmering water.

5 Add the chopped parsley to the sauce and serve with the salmon rolls.

Per portion Energy 694kcal/2867kJ; Protein 25.7g; Carbohydrate 2.4g, of which sugars 2.1g; Fat 62.5g, of which saturates 33.4g; Cholesterol 187mg; Calcium 55mg; Fibre 0.6g; Sodium 362mg.

Serves 4

1–2 cooked lobsters, 300g/11oz cooked prawns (shrimp) in their shell, or white and brown meat of 1–2 cooked crabs

30–45ml/2–3 tbsp shellfish butter (see below)

30ml/2 tbsp plain (all-purpose) flour

300ml/½ pint/1¼ cups fish stock

150ml/¼ pint/⅔ cup double (heavy) cream

30ml/2 tbsp brandy

30ml/2 tbsp chopped fresh dill

salt and ground black pepper

For the shellfish butter

shells from 1 of the above shellfish

40g/1½oz/3 tbsp butter

For the spinach ring

butter, for greasing

500g/1¼lb fresh spinach leaves, washed, or 225g/8oz frozen chopped spinach, thawed

4 large eggs

200ml/7fl oz/scant 1 cup milk

200ml/7fl oz/scant 1 cup single (light) cream

pinch of grated nutmeg

pinch of ground allspice

salt and ground black pepper

Creamed shellfish in a spinach ring
Skalldyrstuing med spinatrand

Shellfish from the North Sea are greatly loved in Norway. Lobster, prawns and crabs all form part of a cold table or are used in a variety of soups and sauces. The mixture that follows can be served with rice, used as a filling for pastry or an omelette or, as in this recipe, as the filling for a spinach ring.

1 Remove the flesh from the shellfish and cut, if necessary, into bitesize pieces. Keep the flesh in the refrigerator for use later and reserve the shells for the shellfish butter.

2 To make the shellfish butter, using a mortar and pestle, pound the reserved shells thoroughly. Add the butter and work into the shell fragments. Put the mixture in a pan and cook over a low heat for 15 minutes, without browning. Add water to just cover the shells, bring to the boil then reduce the heat and simmer for 1 minute.

3 Strain the liquid through a fine sieve (strainer) and leave to cool. When cold, put the liquid in the refrigerator and leave until the butter has set on the surface, about 2–3 hours.

4 Preheat the oven to 180°C/350°F/Gas 4. Lift the butter off the surface of the liquid.

5 Generously butter a 1 litre/1¾ pint ring mould. If using fresh spinach, plunge it into a pan of boiling water then drain immediately. Refresh under cold running water, drain and squeeze until the spinach is dry. Chop it finely either by hand or in a blender.

6 Lightly beat the eggs, then add the milk and cream and stir well. Add the spinach and season with the nutmeg, allspice, salt and a little pepper.

7 Pour the mixture into the prepared mould and place it in a roasting pan. Fill with hot water to reach three-quarters of the way up the sides of the mould. Bake in the oven for about 35 minutes or until the tip of a knife, inserted in the ring, comes out clean.

8 Meanwhile, make the creamed shellfish. Melt the shellfish butter in a pan, stir in the flour and cook over a low heat for 1–2 minutes, without colouring. Remove from the heat and gradually stir in the fish stock to form a smooth sauce. Stir in the cream. Return to the heat and, stirring all the time, cook until the sauce boils and thickens. Simmer over a low heat for 2–3 minutes.

9 Add the brandy to the sauce and season with salt and pepper. Add the reserved shellfish and heat gently, without boiling, until heated through. Stir in the chopped dill.

10 When the spinach ring is cooked, leave to stand for 2–3 minutes, then run a knife around the edge of the mould and invert the ring on to a serving plate. Fill the centre with the creamed shellfish and serve hot.

Per portion Energy 620kcal/2573kJ; Protein 34.5g; Carbohydrate 12g, of which sugars 6.1g; Fat 46.9g, of which saturates 26.3g; Cholesterol 393mg; Calcium 431mg; Fibre 2.9g; Sodium 650mg.

Serves 4

115g/4oz/1¾ cups mushrooms, sliced

juice ½ lemon

1 lobster, about 450g/1lb, cooked and with meat extracted

115g/4oz/1 cup cooked fresh or canned asparagus

1 crisp lettuce, shredded

16 cooked mussels

115g/4oz/½ cup cooked peeled prawns (shrimp)

2 tomatoes, skinned and quartered

dill fronds, to garnish

For the dressing

30ml/2 tbsp white wine vinegar

90–120ml/6–8 tbsp olive oil

pinch of sugar

1 garlic clove, crushed (optional)

salt and ground black pepper

Shellfish salad
Skalldyrsalat

This salad was created to take full advantage of the many types of delicious shellfish that can be caught off the west coast of Norway. It appears on all Norwegian cold tables for special occasions, with the shellfish chosen according to its availability and taste. When fresh shellfish is scarce or prohibitively expensive, frozen or canned is an alternative.

1 Chill all the salad ingredients in the refrigerator before use. To make the dressing, put the vinegar, oil, sugar and garlic, if using, in a bowl and mix well together. Season the dressing with salt and pepper to taste.

2 Put the mushrooms in a serving bowl and sprinkle over the lemon juice. Cut the lobster meat into bitesize pieces and add to the bowl. Cut the fresh or canned asparagus into 5cm/2in pieces and add to the bowl. Add the lettuce in a layer, the mussels, prawns and tomatoes.

3 Pour the dressing over the salad ingredients and toss together. Garnish with dill fronds and serve immediately.

Per portion Energy 280kcal/1166kJ; Protein 23.2g; Carbohydrate 4.4g, of which sugars 3g; Fat 19g, of which saturates 2.9g; Cholesterol 127mg; Calcium 96mg; Fibre 1.8g; Sodium 357mg.

Fish mousse
Fiskepudding

This delicious fish mousse is filled with creamed shellfish, which is also used in the recipe that fills a spinach ring. It makes a superb appetizer for a dinner party, or alternatively it can be prepared as a filling main dish.

1 Preheat the oven to 190°C/375°F/Gas 5. Generously butter a 1 litre/1¾ pint ring mould and sprinkle with the breadcrumbs to coat, then tap out the excess crumbs. Put the flour and egg yolks in a bowl, then beat in the single cream until smooth.

2 Put the fish and anchovy fillet in a blender or food processor and blend in the flour mixture. Season the mixture with salt and pepper and return it to the bowl.

3 Pour the double cream into a bowl and whisk until it just holds its shape. Fold the cream into the fish mixture. In a clean bowl, whisk the egg whites until they form soft peaks and then fold into the fish mixture.

4 Transfer the fish mixture to the prepared mould. Cover with buttered foil and place the mould in a roasting pan. Fill the tin with hot water to reach three-quarters of the way up the sides of the mould. Bake in the oven for about 40 minutes until the mousse is firm and slightly risen.

5 When the fish mousse is cooked, leave to stand for 2–3 minutes, then run a knife around the edge of the mould and invert the ring on to a serving plate. Fill the centre with creamed shellfish, garnish with dill and serve hot.

Per portion Energy 203kcal/845kJ; Protein 9.3g; Carbohydrate 11.8g, of which sugars 1g; Fat 13.5g, of which saturates 7.7g; Cholesterol 92mg; Calcium 54mg; Fibre 0.4g; Sodium 144mg.

Serves 6–8 as an appetizer, 4 as a main dish

butter, for greasing

60–70ml/4–5 tbsp fine dry breadcrumbs, for coating

25ml/1½ tbsp plain (all-purpose) flour

2 large eggs, separated

150ml/¼ pint/⅔ cup single (light) cream

225g/8oz fish, such as hake or coley, skinned

1 anchovy fillet

120ml/4fl oz/½ cup double (heavy) cream

salt and ground black pepper

dill fronds, to garnish

creamed shellfish, to serve (see page 57)

Variation The prawns (shrimp) in the creamed shellfish recipe could be replaced with asparagus tips.

Chef's-style klipfish
Kokkens klippfisk

Klipfish is another name for salt cod. Nowadays, there is no need to salt cod to preserve it, but the taste for traditional dishes with this ingredient remain. The following recipe for a tasty casserole draws on the salted cod tradition, and is a new interpretation of an idea by the Norwegian chef, Harold Osa.

1 Soak the cod in cold water for two days, changing the water at least three times a day. Drain and remove the skin and bones, then cut the fish into thin slices.

2 Put the leeks and carrots in a pan and add enough water to just cover. Add the cream and season with salt and pepper. Bring to the boil then lower the heat and simmer for about 10 minutes, until tender. Bring to the boil and boil for a further 2–3 minutes, then remove from the heat and leave to cool.

3 Put the bacon in a frying pan and fry until the fat starts to melt.

4 Preheat the oven to 200°C/400°F/Gas 6. Grease an ovenproof dish. Layer the cooled vegetables with the cod slices in the dish, starting and ending with the vegetables. Sprinkle the bacon over the top. Bake in the oven for about 15 minutes. Serve hot, with boiled potatoes.

Per portion Energy 609kcal/2556kJ; Protein 93.1g; Carbohydrate 6.1g, of which sugars 5.2g; Fat 23.7g, of which saturates 9.5g; Cholesterol 204mg; Calcium 98mg; Fibre 3.1g; Sodium 1801mg.

Serves 4

1kg/2¼lb salt cod

450g/1lb leeks, white and pale green parts only, thinly sliced

150g/5oz carrots, thinly sliced

45ml/3 tbsp double (heavy) cream

250g/9oz rindless, unsmoked, thick cut streaky (fatty) bacon, cut into small pieces

salt and ground black pepper

boiled potatoes, to serve

Cook's tip Use bacon dry-cured in the old fashioned way, as bacon cured by modern methods may produce too much liquid during frying.

Serves 4

1kg/2¼lb salt cod

about 500g/1¼lb potatoes, sliced

1 onion, sliced

100ml/3½fl oz/scant ½ cup water

100ml/3½fl oz/scant ½ cup olive oil

75ml/2½fl oz/⅓ cup strained tomatoes

a little chopped red chilli

Cook's tip It helps to have two sharp knives for preparing the cod; a small one to cut away the flesh from the bones, and a larger, flexible-bladed one to slide, in a sawing motion, between the flesh and the skin. A little salt on the fingers will help to grip the skin.

Salted cod casserole
Bacalao

Bacalao is a type of dried and salted fish used in Portugal and Spain, but in Norway it means a casserole made from salt cod, tomatoes, potatoes and oil. This dish is a particular favourite in the salt-fish ports of Kristiansund and Alesund.

1 Soak the cod in cold water for two days, changing the water at least three times a day. Drain and remove the skin and bones, then cut the fish into pieces measuring about 5cm/2in square.

2 Layer the fish, potatoes and finally the onion in a medium flameproof casserole. Put the water, oil, strained tomatoes and the chilli in a pan and bring to the boil. Pour into the casserole.

3 Return the liquid to the boil, reduce the heat, cover and simmer for 1½–2 hours, until the potatoes are tender.

Per portion Energy 590kcal/2484kJ; Protein 83.7g; Carbohydrate 21.9g, of which sugars 3.1g; Fat 19.2g, of which saturates 3g; Cholesterol 148mg; Calcium 68mg; Fibre 1.7g; Sodium 1016mg.

Fish for a prince
Prinsefisk

This classic Norwegian fish dish is a speciality of Bergen and is perfect to serve on a special occasion. Each of the ingredients should be of prime quality with excellent flavour, but it is the colours of the white fish, green asparagus and seafood garnish that makes the dish particularly attractive and fit for a royal table.

1 Preheat the oven to 190°C/375°F/Gas 5. Cut the fish into four serving portions. Put in an ovenproof dish and pour over enough fish stock to cover. Bake in the oven for 10–15 minutes, until just tender.

2 Meanwhile, steam the asparagus spears for 6–8 minutes, according to their size, until tender.

3 When cooked, carefully transfer the fish to a serving dish, reserving the stock, and keep warm. Pour the stock through a sieve (strainer).

4 Melt the butter in a pan, stir in the flour and cook over a low heat for 1–2 minutes, without colouring. Remove from the heat and gradually stir in the fish stock to form a smooth sauce. Add the cream.

5 Return the pan to the heat and, stirring all the time, cook until the sauce boils and thickens. Simmer over a low heat for 2–3 minutes. Add a squeeze of lemon juice and the sherry and season to taste with salt and pepper.

6 Pour a little of the sauce over each piece of fish. Garnish the dish with the prawns or crayfish tails and the asparagus spears and sprinkle each fish with a little chopped parsley. Serve hot, accompanied by the remaining sauce.

Serves 4

600g/1⅓lb piece boneless, skinned cod or halibut fillet

about 475ml/16fl oz/2 cups fish stock

8 asparagus spears

40g/1½oz/3 tbsp butter

40g/1½oz/3 tbsp plain (all-purpose) flour

120ml/4fl oz/½ cup double (heavy) cream

A squeeze of lemon juice

45ml/3 tbsp medium dry sherry

150g/5oz/½ cup peeled cooked prawns (shrimp), with tails on, or 4 large crayfish tails

salt and ground black pepper

chopped fresh parsley, to garnish

Cook's tip Serving on individual plates controls the size of each portion but, if you prefer, all the ingredients can be arranged on an attractive large dish.

Per portion Energy 425kcal/1769kJ; Protein 36.3g; Carbohydrate 9.5g, of which sugars 1.9g; Fat 25.9g, of which saturates 15.5g; Cholesterol 205mg; Calcium 81mg; Fibre 0.7g; Sodium 232mg.

Serves 4

50g/2oz/½ cup plain (all-purpose) flour

675g/1½lb pollock fillet, skinned and cut into 4 serving portions

50g/2oz/4 tbsp butter

15ml/1 tbsp vegetable oil

2 large onions, sliced

5ml/1 tsp sugar

200ml/7fl oz/scant 1 cup water

salt and ground black pepper

To serve

boiled potatoes

a green vegetable, such as cabbage

Pollock with onions
Lyr med løk

Pollock is a favourite, less expensive alternative to cod and it is often served along the Norwegian coast. The flesh is much firmer than cod and has a slightly pearly hue. It is full of flavour and forms a delicious partnership with the fried onions that feature in this dish.

1 Preheat the oven to 180°C/350°F/Gas 4. Put the flour on a large plate and season with salt and pepper. Dip the fish portions in the flour to coat on both sides. Put a knob of the butter and the oil in a large frying pan and heat until the butter has melted. Add the floured fish and fry quickly on both sides until browned. Place in an ovenproof dish.

2 Melt the remaining butter in the same pan, add the onions, season with salt and pepper and fry gently for about 10 minutes until softened and golden brown. Add the sugar, increase the heat and allow the onion to caramelise slightly.

3 Spread the onions over the fish. Add the water to the frying pan, stirring to lift any sediment on the bottom of the pan, bring to the boil then pour over the fish and onions. Bake in the oven for about 20 minutes, until the fish is tender.

4 Serve with boiled potatoes and a green vegetable.

Per portion Energy 298kcal/1247kJ; Protein 32.9g; Carbohydrate 16g, of which sugars 5g; Fat 11.8g, of which saturates 6.7g; Cholesterol 104mg; Calcium 52mg; Fibre 1.3g; Sodium 180mg.

Crisp fried herrings
Sprøstekt sild

Herrings are an integral part of Norwegian cuisine. Salted herrings are essential on any Norwegian cold table and fresh herrings, crisply fried as in this recipe, are a welcome feature of any meal.

1 Rinse the herring fillets under cold water and dry on kitchen paper. Put the flour on a plate and season with salt and pepper. Break the egg and beat in lightly. Spread the breadcrumbs on another plate. Dip the fish fillets in the flour, to coat on both sides, then into the beaten egg and then the breadcrumbs.

2 Melt the butter in a large frying pan, add the coated fillets and fry over a medium heat for about 3–4 minutes on each side, until golden brown.

3 Serve with mustard sauce or sour cream and pickled beetroot, boiled potatoes and a green vegetable.

Per portion Energy 427kcal/1788kJ; Protein 23.9g; Carbohydrate 32.1g, of which sugars 1g; Fat 23.5g, of which saturates 8.9g; Cholesterol 119mg; Calcium 124mg; Fibre 1g; Sodium 417mg.

Serves 4

4 herrings, filleted

50g/2oz/⅓ cup plain (all-purpose) flour

1 egg

115g/4oz/2 cups fine dried breadcrumbs

40g/1½oz/3 tbsp butter

salt and ground black pepper

To serve

mustard sauce (see page 27) or sour cream and pickled beetroot (beet) (see page 30)

boiled potatoes

a green vegetable, such as spinach

Domestic
meat

Lamb in buttermillk with roasted
   shell potatoes

Lamb and cabbage

Lamb fricassée

Beef meatballs in gravy

Fried pork and apples

Roast pork loin with red
   cabbage

Norwegian beef stew

Braised chicken with mashed
   swede

Casseroles, crackling, braising and roasts

The temperate climate of Norway's coastal regions and islands produces rich pastures. As with other Scandinavian countries, there is little or no pollution, imports are strictly controlled and pesticides and antibiotics are rarely used. This ensures that Norway produces meat with a wonderful flavour.

Historically, Norwegians could not afford much meat. When they did indulge in a joint or a casserole, they liked to prepare it in a simple, unelaborate way. Beef is the main ingredient of Norway's version of the famous Scandinavian meatballs, kjøttkaker. Roast pork is a prized joint that often provides the Christmas celebration dish, although more and more Norwegians today choose turkey.

Smoking meat was a way of helping to preserve it in the days before modern refrigeration techniques. A leg of pork could be soaked in brine and hung in the chimney, producing a ham that could be served hot or cold. The same could be done with a leg of lamb, and many Norwegians think that smoked lamb has a superior flavour to ham.

When it was time to slaughter animals in the autumn, Norwegian households sat down to a meat dish called fårikål. Made with lamb and cabbage, this casserole is the nearest thing to a national dish. The dish was most often made of mutton, for only the wealthy could afford lamb. Nowadays, however, lamb is enjoyed by most of the population.

Chickens have always been kept for egg laying. At the end of its life, a hen can be cooked slowly to provide a casserole or fricassée. A chicken raised for the table was a real treat and Norwegians have a special method of braising chicken, included in this chapter.

Lamb in buttermilk with roasted shell potatoes
Lammelår i surmelk med potetmos i skallet

This recipe shows how marinating meat was a good way of keeping it fresh, although only if the intention wasn't to keep the meat for too long. Today, lamb is still marinated in buttermilk, natural yogurt or sour milk. It makes the meat very moist and tender and gives it a sweet flavour. The potatoes are a simple but delicious variation on baked potatoes. The preparation can be done beforehand and the filled potatoes reheated in the oven with the lamb.

Serves 4–6

1 leg of lamb, knuckle end trimmed, total weight about 2kg/4½lb

3.5–4.8 litres/6–8 pints/15–20 cups buttermilk or natural (plain) yogurt

15ml/1 tbsp salt

250ml/8fl oz/1 cup water

For the sauce

600ml/1 pint/2½ cups chicken or vegetable stock

5ml/1 tsp potato flour

150ml/¼ pint/⅔ cup sour cream

salt and ground black pepper

To serve

a green vegetable, such as green beans

rowan jelly or cranberry sauce

For the potatoes

4–6 baking potatoes

50–75g/2–3oz/4–6 tbsp butter

45–60ml/3–4 tbsp double (heavy) cream

1 bunch spring onions (scallions), white and pale green parts only, chopped

45ml/3 tbsp grated Jarlsberg cheese

salt and ground black pepper

Variation Instead of the sauce, the natural juices from the lamb, with a little stock, can be served with the meat.

1 Put the leg of lamb in a large bowl and add enough buttermilk or natural yogurt to cover the meat. Keep in the refrigerator for 4–6 days, turning the meat three or four times a day.

2 To prepare the potatoes, preheat the oven to 200°C/400°F/Gas 6. Prick the potatoes all over with a fork and bake in the oven for 1 hour until tender.

3 Cut a slice off the top of each potato and scoop out the insides into a bowl, leaving a sturdy shell. Add the butter to the cooked potato and mash well together. Add the cream and spring onions, and season to taste with salt and pepper. Replace the cooked potato inside the potato shells and top with the grated cheese.

4 When ready to cook the lamb, preheat the oven to 160°C/325°F/Gas 3. Remove the meat from the buttermilk or yogurt, dry on kitchen paper and rub with salt. Place in a roasting pan, standing on a rack, and pour the water into the roasting pan. Roast in the oven for about 1½ hours until tender. A meat thermometer should read 76°C/169°F and the meat should only just be cooked. During cooking, keep the water in the roasting pan topped up.

5 About 20 minutes before the lamb is cooked, arrange the potato shells on a baking tray and reheat in the oven until hot.

6 When the lamb is cooked, remove the meat from the pan, transfer to a warmed serving dish, cover with foil and leave in a warm place while preparing the sauce.

7 Add a little of the stock to the roasting pan, stirring to deglaze the pan and scraping up any sediment from the bottom of the pan. Add enough of the remaining stock to make up to about 1.2 litre/2 pints/5 cups in total. Pour the juices through a sieve (strainer) into a large pan.

8 In a small bowl, blend the potato flour with a little cold water to form a smooth paste and add a little of the hot liquid. Stir into the pan and heat, stirring until thickened. Remove from the heat before it boils and stir in the sour cream. Season with salt and pepper to taste. Serve the lamb with the sauce, the potatoes, a green vegetable and rowan jelly or cranberry sauce.

Per portion Energy 634kcal/2637kJ; Protein 41.8g; Carbohydrate 12.8g, of which sugars 2.5g; Fat 46.3g, of which saturates 20.9g; Cholesterol 195mg; Calcium 102mg; Fibre 1g; Sodium 235mg.

Lamb and cabbage
Fårikål

This casserole is almost a national dish. A Fårikål Day is celebrated in the autumn and the dish is loved by every Norwegian. It doesn't matter which cut of lamb is used; in poorer times it was the scrag end; now, in better times, shoulder or cutlets are the choice. Whatever cut is used, the combination of sweet lamb and cabbage is comforting and delicious. The peppercorns yield their fierceness in the cooking and add a pleasant punch to the taste.

1 Using a large flameproof casserole and starting with the cabbage, put the cabbage and lamb in layers, sprinkling each of the layers with flour, if using, salt and peppercorns.

2 Pour over enough boiling water to cover both the cabbage and lamb. Bring the casserole to the boil, and then reduce the heat and simmer over a low heat for about 1½ hours, until the meat is tender. Serve very hot on warmed plates, accompanied with boiled potatoes.

Per portion Energy 390kcal/1630kJ; Protein 37.6g; Carbohydrate 16.3g, of which sugars 15.9g; Fat 19.6g, of which saturates 8.8g; Cholesterol 128mg; Calcium 173mg; Fibre 6.8g; Sodium 168mg.

Serves 4

1.5kg/3¼lb cabbage, cored and cut into large wedges

675g/1½lb boneless lamb such as shoulder, fillet or lean breast, cut into large pieces

15–30ml/1–2 tbsp plain (all-purpose) flour (optional)

salt

15ml/1 tbsp black peppercorns

300–450ml/½–¾ pint/1¼–scant 2 cups boiling water

boiled potatoes, to serve

Variation Using stock instead of water adds flavour and, for additional flavour, some cooks include caraway seeds with the peppercorns.

Serves 4–6

1.2kg/2½lb boneless piece of shoulder or breast of lamb

5ml/1 heaped tsp salt per 1 litre/ 1¾ pint/4 cups of water

For the vegetables

2 carrots, peeled and sliced obliquely

115g/4oz green beans, trimmed and cut in half

115g/4oz peas

small cauliflower, trimmed and cut into medium-sized florets

For the sauce

40g/1½ oz/3 tbsp butter

50g/2oz/½ cup plain (all-purpose) flour

750ml/1¼ pints/3 cups stock

salt and ground black pepper

To serve

15ml/1 tbsp chopped parsley

boiled potatoes or rice

Lamb fricassée
Lambe frikasse

This shows a technique of gently simmering meat. When combined with the sauce and vegetables, the fricassée retains the freshness of the individual ingredients.

1 Place the meat in a pan and cover it with water. Remove the meat and add salt according to the amount of water. Bring the water to the boil, then add the meat. Bring the liquid back to the boil, then skim off any froth and lower the heat until the water does no more than quiver. Cook for 2½ hours or until tender.

2 Cook the vegetables individually in salted water, leaving them slightly underdone. Drain and refresh in cold water. Once the meat is cooked, leave it in the stock.

3 Melt the butter, stir in the flour and cook gently for 2 minutes. Skim fat from the stock, then gradually add to the butter and flour, stirring until the sauce is smooth and thickened. Season to taste. Simmer gently for 2–3 minutes.

4 Pour boiling water over the vegetables to reheat and cut the meat into bitesize pieces. Place the lamb in a serving dish, add the drained vegetables, pour over the sauce, garnish with the chopped parsley and serve with boiled potatoes or rice.

Per portion Energy 496kcal/2072kJ; Protein 44.9g; Carbohydrate 14.4g, of which sugars 5.6g; Fat 29.2g, of which saturates 14.2g; Cholesterol 166mg; Calcium 66mg; Fibre 3.9g; Sodium 229mg.

500g/1¼lb finely minced (ground) beef

large pinch of grated nutmeg

large pinch of ground allspice

large pinch of ground ginger

15ml/1 tbsp potato flour

200ml/7fl oz/scant 1 cup milk or water

1 egg, lightly beaten

30ml/2 tbsp vegetable oil

25g/1oz/2 tbsp butter

25g/1oz plain (all-purpose) flour

600ml/1 pint/2½ cups beef stock

30–45ml/2–3 tbsp double (heavy) cream

salt and ground black pepper

Beef meatballs in gravy
Kjøttkaker med kålstuing

This is the Norwegian version of meatballs, although everyone has their own recipe. Traditionally made with beef, some cooks will use a mixture of beef and pork, while others will add finely chopped onions or vary the seasonings.

1 Put the minced beef in a bowl and add the grated nutmeg, ground allspice, ground ginger, potato flour, 5ml/1 tsp salt and pepper and beat well. Add the milk or water, little by little, beating after each addition. Add the beaten egg and beat well again.

2 With wet hands, shape the mixture into balls. (The balls can be any size you like but the larger the balls, the longer it will take to cook them.)

3 Heat the oil in a large frying pan, add the meatballs and fry over a medium heat until cooked. If necessary, fry them in batches. Remove them and transfer to a plate.

4 When the meatballs are cooked, add the butter and heat until melted. Add the flour, stirring to deglaze the pan, scraping up any sediment. Gradually add the stock, stirring all the time to form a smooth sauce. When all the stock has been added, bring slowly to the boil, stirring, until the sauce boils and thickens. Check the seasonings, adding salt and pepper only if necessary, then simmer for 10 minutes.

5 Add the cream to the sauce, then add the meatballs and simmer for a further 10 minutes. Serve hot.

Per portion Energy 454kcal/1882kJ; Protein 26.9g; Carbohydrate 5g, of which sugars 0.3g; Fat 36.4g, of which saturates 15.5g; Cholesterol 146mg; Calcium 32mg; Fibre 0.2g; Sodium 157mg.

Fried pork and apples
Epleflesk

This is a very simple dish that turns an inexpensive cut of meat into a most enjoyable meal. It is ideal for a quick supper dish. Norwegian apples are very crisp and have a beautiful flavour; the summer may not be long but the days are filled with almost 24 hours of sunshine, which helps the fruit to ripen.

1 Heat a large frying pan, without any oil or fat, until hot. Add the pork slices and fry over a low heat, 3–4 minutes each side, until golden brown. Season the pork slices with salt and pepper. Transfer to a warmed serving dish and keep warm.

2 Core the apples but do not peel, then cut the apples into rings. Add the apple rings to the frying pan and fry gently in the pork fat, 3–4 minutes each side, until just beginning to turn golden and translucent. Sprinkle the slices with the sugar and turn once more for a couple of minutes until the sugar side starts to caramelize. Serve the pork slices with the apple rings. Accompany with boiled potatoes and a green vegetable, garnished with parsley.

Per portion Energy 645kcal/2676kJ; Protein 23.4g; Carbohydrate 19g, of which sugars 19g; Fat 53.4g, of which saturates 19.7g; Cholesterol 108mg; Calcium 21mg; Fibre 2g; Sodium 113mg.

Serves 4

600g/1¼lb lightly salted or fresh belly of pork, cut into thin slices

500g/1¼lb crisp eating apples

30ml/2 tbsp soft light brown sugar

salt and ground black pepper

chopped fresh parsley or chives, to garnish

To serve

boiled potatoes

a green vegetable

Cook's tip Cut the apple rings to a depth of 5mm/¼in across the apple. Most apples will make 4 rings.

Roast pork loin with red cabbage
Svinestek med rødkål

A roast pork loin, served with red cabbage, is a Norwegian Christmas festive dish. The rind of the pork is scored into squares and for this the Norwegians have special knives, although a butcher can do this for you. There is much competition amongst Norwegian cooks to achieve a really crisp crackling.

1 To prepare the pork, rub the pork rind with salt and pepper. Put in the refrigerator and leave for 24 hours or even a little longer.

2 To prepare the red cabbage, melt the butter in a large flameproof casserole or pan. Add the shredded cabbage, apples and caraway seeds, if using, salt and pepper and fry gently, tossing the ingredients together until well mixed and coated in butter. Take care not to allow the cabbage to catch on the bottom of the pan.

3 Add the vinegar and water to the pan, cover and cook gently for 2 hours until the cabbage is tender. Add the jelly and sugar to taste. The cabbage is better if allowed to cool, kept in the refrigerator overnight and reheated the following day.

4 When ready to cook the pork, preheat the oven to 240°C/475°F/Gas 9. Put the loin, rind side down, in a roasting pan and add the water. Cover with foil and put in the oven for 20 minutes.

5 Reduce the oven temperature to 180°C/350°F/Gas 4. Remove the foil, turn the meat rind side up, and roast for 1½ hours. Increase the heat to 230°C/450°F/Gas 8 and roast for a further 20 minutes, until the crackling is crisp. If not, roast for about a further 20 minutes, but do not over-cook the meat.

6 Meanwhile, turn the red cabbage into a flameproof casserole or pan. Some 20 minutes before serving, gently reheat the cabbage. Serve the cooked pork with the red cabbage, roast potatoes, glazed onions and a green salad.

Per portion Energy 416kcal/1749kJ; Protein 55.8g; Carbohydrate 20g, of which sugars 19.8g; Fat 12.9g, of which saturates 5.1g; Cholesterol 164mg; Calcium 96mg; Fibre 3.8g; Sodium 209mg.

Serves 6–8

2kg/4½lb pork loin, rind scored into 2.5cm/1in squares

500ml/17fl oz/generous 2 cups water

salt and ground black pepper

For the red cabbage

25g/1oz/2 tbsp butter

1 red cabbage, total weight about 1.2kg/2½lb, cored and finely sliced

2 cooking apples, peeled, cored and diced

15ml/1 tbsp caraway seeds (optional)

90ml/6 tbsp cider vinegar

150ml/¼ pint/⅔ cup water

60ml/4 tbsp rowan or redcurrant jelly

30–45ml/2–3 tbsp sugar

salt and ground black pepper

To serve

roast potatoes

glazed onions (see page 64)

green salad

Cook's tip As well as serving red cabbage with the Christmas roast pork, it is also good served with any pork dish or roast game and birds, such as duck or goose.

Norwegian beef stew
Lapskaus

A traditional Norwegian casserole of beef cooked with root vegetables makes this a complete meal in a pot. Cooking the vegetables separately from the meat for part of the time is an interesting technique, which allows them to keep more of their own flavour than would be possible if added to the meat at the beginning.

1 Put the beef in a large pan, add enough water to cover, season with salt and pepper and bring slowly to the boil. Lower the heat, cover and simmer for 1 hour.

2 When the beef has been cooking for 30 minutes, bring the stock to the boil in a flameproof casserole. Add the carrots and swede or turnip and simmer for 15 minutes. Add the potatoes and simmer for a further 15 minutes.

3 When the beef has been cooking for 1 hour, strain the cubes, reserving the stock for a soup or another dish. Add the beef to the vegetables with the onion. Check the seasoning, adding salt and pepper only if necessary.

4 Simmer the casserole for a further 15–30 minutes, depending on the quality of the meat, until the meat and vegetables are tender. Serve hot.

Per portion Energy 475kcal/1987kJ; Protein 48.4g; Carbohydrate 28.2g, of which sugars 10.8g; Fat 19.4g, of which saturates 7.8g; Cholesterol 116mg; Calcium 73mg; Fibre 4.3g; Sodium 170mg.

Serves 4-6

1.2kg/2½lb stewing beef, cut into large cubes

1.2 litres/2 pints/5 cups beef stock

450g/1lb carrots, cut into bitesize pieces

1 small swede (rutabaga) or turnip

675g/1½lb potatoes, cut into bitesize pieces

1 onion, finely chopped

salt and ground black pepper

Cook's tip Try to select beef with a marbling of fat running through it as this will give a moister, more tender result than a very lean cut of meat.

Serves 4

75g/3oz/6 tbsp butter

1 small bunch fresh parsley

1.6kg/3½lb chicken

salt and ground black pepper

For the mashed swede (rutabaga)

450g/1lb swedes (rutabaga), cut into cubes

675g/1½lb potatoes, cut into cubes

about 115g/4oz/½ cup butter

pinch of ground allspice

salt and ground black pepper

Braised chicken with mashed swede
Stekt kylling med kålrotstuing

This traditional way of cooking chicken maintains maximum flavour and produces delicious juices in the dish. It is served with a mixture of mashed swede and potato, both absorbing the butter to give a creamy purée.

1 Put the butter, parsley, salt and pepper inside the chicken. Heat the oil and the rest of the butter in a flameproof casserole. Add the chicken and brown on all sides. Season.

2 Lower the heat, cover the pan and simmer gently for 1 hour. Test by inserting the point of a sharp knife into the thigh near the body until the juices are clear.

3 Prepare the mashed swede. Put the swede in a large pan, cover with water and season with salt. Bring to the boil, lower the heat and simmer for 15 minutes.

4 Add the potatoes to the pan of swedes and simmer for 15 minutes. Drain, reserving a little water and return the vegetables to the pan. Mash well, then add the butter and allspice. Season the mashed vegetables with salt and pepper.

5 When cooked, transfer the chicken to a warmed serving dish. Add a little water to the pan to make a simple gravy, stirring to deglaze the pan and scraping up any sediment from the bottom. Serve the chicken with the gravy and mashed swede.

Per portion Energy 821kcal/3410kJ; Protein 43.5g; Carbohydrate 33g, of which sugars 7.9g; Fat 58g, of which saturates 24.9g; Cholesterol 269mg; Calcium 91mg; Fibre 3.8g; Sodium 372mg.

Game

Saddle of roe deer with glazed
carrots

Reindeer terrine with juniper
berries and aquavit

Roe deer medallions with
redcurrants

Braised venison with roasted
root vegetables

Pheasant stuffed with mountain
fruits

Quail in cream sauce

Roast hare with lingonberries

From grouse to red deer – nature's game pantry

In a country such as Norway that has so little agricultural land and such a short growing season, hunting has always made a valuable contribution to the task of survival. Today there is not the same need to hunt to secure an adequate diet – the use of the freezer, in particular, means that food is easily available throughout the year – and yet hunting is now as popular in Norway as it ever was. The main hunting season takes place in late autumn, and is very much a part of everyday life, with participants also taking pleasure in the majestic countryside, the awe-inspiring scenery and the pure and invigorating air.

The chief animals that are hunted are elk (moose), reindeer (caribou) and roe deer, red deer and fallow deer. Reindeer are found in many districts and the desolately beautiful Hardangervidda plateau, with its tundra landscape that links east and west Norway, is home to Europe's largest herd of reindeer.

The season for hare (jack rabbit) and ptarmigan lasts into February. Hare has not always been popular, but its merits as a table meat are well appreciated today. Ptarmigan has a ready market and hunters have often been able to supplement their income by trapping or shooting more birds than they need. Other game includes black grouse and wood grouse.

If you are lucky enough to have hunted your own meat, then adapt your preparation technique to suit its age and condition. Older specimens need marinating and slow cooking to ensure tenderness – the Reindeer Terrine with Juniper Berries and Aquavit recipe is ideal for cuts such as these. Young game is much more tender and can be roasted with delicious results. Remember, however, that the flesh will continue cooking after being removed from the heat, so always take it from the oven underdone to avoid overcooking.

Serves 6

2kg/4½lb saddle of venison, preferably roe deer, boned, with bones reserved

1 carrot

1 small leek

1 celery stick

½ onion

1 bunch fresh parsley

75–100g/3–4oz/6–8 tbsp unsalted butter, softened

120ml/4fl oz/½ cup red wine

5ml/1 tsp potato flour or arrowroot

15ml/1 tbsp water

300ml/½ pint/1¼ cups whipping cream or sour cream

salt and ground black pepper

For the glazed carrots

475ml/16fl oz/2 cups water

9 carrots, each cut into 4 pieces

75g/3oz/6 tbsp butter

1½ tbsp sugar

1½ tsp salt

chopped fresh parsley, to garnish

To serve

boiled potatoes

glazed onions (see page 64)

a green vegetable

rowan or redcurrant jelly

Cook's tips

• Underneath the saddle are slim little fillets. Reserve these for another occasion by slicing and cooking in a quick stir-fry with mushrooms and, perhaps, celery.

• If using potato flour in step 6, do not allow the mixture to re-boil or the sauce may go stringy.

Saddle of roe deer with glazed carrots
Rådyrsadel med glaserte gulerøtter

The saddle of roe deer is the choicest cut, yielding two lengths of tenderloin. There is no waste and the meat is tender and melts in the mouth. The saddle of larger deer can be cooked in the same way but allow longer for the roasting.

1 Put the reserved meat bones in a large pan with the carrot, leek, celery, onion and parsley, salt and pepper. Add water to cover, bring to the boil, simmer for 1½–2 hours, then strain, skim off any fat, then reserve 600ml/1 pint/2½ cups of the stock.

2 To prepare the carrots, boil the water in a pan. Add the carrots, butter, sugar and salt, return to the boil and cook, uncovered, for 40 minutes until the water has almost evaporated. Shake the pan occasionally to coat the carrots in the glaze.

3 Preheat the oven to 200°C/400°F/Gas 6. Slip a small, sharp knife underneath the membrane on the saddle and remove it. Trim the meat of all sinews and gristle. Heat 25g/1oz/2 tbsp of the butter in a flameproof casserole, add the meat and fry until brown. Season and spread the remaining 50g/2oz/4 tbsp of butter over the meat.

4 Place the meat on a rack in a roasting pan and roast for 10–15 minutes. Press the meat to test how well cooked it is – it should be slightly underdone and should give slightly when pressed, as it will continue to cook after being removed from the oven. Transfer to a warmed serving dish, cover with foil and leave to rest for 15–20 minutes.

5 Pour the wine into a pan, bring to the boil and boil until reduced by half. In a small bowl, blend the potato flour or arrowroot with the water to form a smooth paste.

6 Add the reserved stock to the roasting pan, stirring to deglaze the pan and scraping up any sediment. Strain the juices into a pan and add the reduced wine. Add a little hot liquid to the flour paste and stir into the pan. Bring to the boil, stirring until thickened. Add the cream and reheat gently, not allowing the mixture to boil. Season if necessary.

7 Serve the meat cut into thick slices with the sauce, the carrots garnished with chopped parsley, boiled potatoes, glazed onions, a green vegetable and rowan jelly.

Per portion Energy 576kcal/2390kJ; Protein 31.4g; Carbohydrate 12.9g, of which sugars 12.4g; Fat 43.9g, of which saturates 26.8g; Cholesterol 172mg; Calcium 68mg; Fibre 2.4g; Sodium 264mg.

Serves 6–8

Serves 6–8

500g/1¼lb reindeer or stewing venison, finely chopped

500g/1¼lb fat belly of pork, minced (ground)

10ml/2 tsp chopped fresh thyme

10ml/2 tsp chopped fresh rosemary

6 juniper berries, well crushed

a little grated nutmeg

50ml/2fl oz/¼ cup aquavit or brandy

1 garlic clove

10ml/2 tsp sea salt

1 bay leaf

6–8 slices unsmoked streaky (fatty) bacon, rind removed

200ml/7fl oz/scant 1 cup double (heavy) cream

ground black pepper

Reindeer terrine with juniper berries and aquavit

Rådyrpostei med enerbær og akevitt

This simple stewing venison recipe makes a hearty terrine. It is full of flavour, and is ideal for a picnic or a cold table. Preparation starts a day before cooking and it is best eaten two to three days after making it to allow its flavours to mature.

1 Put the meat, herbs, juniper berries, nutmeg, pepper and aquavit or brandy in a bowl. Crush the garlic with the salt and add to the mixture. Cover and leave in the refrigerator.

2 The next day, preheat the oven to150°C/300°F/Gas 2. Put the bay leaf in the bottom of a 1kg/2¼lb loaf tin (pan). With a knife back, stretch the streaky bacon and line the tin.

3 Add the cream to the meat mixture and mix in well. Turn the mixture into the tin and flip the ends of the bacon slices over the mixture. Place the tin in a roasting pan and fill with hot water to come halfway up the sides of the pan. Bake the terrine in the oven for about 1½ hours or until the terrine starts to come away from the sides of the tin.

4 Remove the tin from the oven and put on a heatproof tray, dish or pan with sides. Place a board on top and weight it down so the juices overflow. Leave the terrine to cool then remove from the tin, wrap in foil and chill in the refrigerator before serving.

Per portion Energy 492kcal/2039kJ; Protein 26.8g; Carbohydrate 0.4g, of which sugars 0.4g; Fat 41.4g, of which saturates 18.6g; Cholesterol 123mg; Calcium 22mg; Fibre 0g; Sodium 322mg.

Serves 6

about 800g/1¾lb venison fillet, preferably roe deer, cut into 8 medallions

15g/½oz/1 tbsp butter

15ml/1 tbsp vegetable oil

salt and ground black pepper

For the sauce

200ml/7fl oz/scant 1 cup venison or beef stock

150ml/¼ pint/⅔ cup port

100ml/3½fl oz/scant ½ cup double (heavy) cream

30ml/2 tbsp redcurrants

a knob of butter

To serve

boiled new potatoes

glazed onions (see page 64)

a green salad

Cook's tip The meat needs to be served slightly underdone, which means the roasted medallions should give slightly when pressed.

Roe deer medallions with redcurrants
Rådyrmedaljonger med rips

This is a dish that should be used for a special occasion. The equivalent cut of beef would be tournedos from the fillet. With venison or roe deer the fillet is much smaller, so ask for the medallions to be cut from the thick end of the fillet and allow two per person.

1 Preheat the oven to 200°C/400°F/Gas 6. Season the venison medallions with salt and pepper. Heat the butter and oil in a large frying pan, add the medallions and quickly sear on both sides, then put on a baking tray and set aside.

2 Add the stock to the pan, stirring to deglaze and scraping up any sediment from the bottom of the pan. Add the port and cream, stir well together, then cook until reduced by half. Season the sauce with salt and pepper to taste. Add the redcurrants and a knob of butter.

3 Roast the medallions in the oven for 4–5 minutes, according to size, until slightly underdone. Place the medallions on individual warmed serving plates or a serving dish, pour a little sauce over each and serve the remaining sauce separately. Accompany with boiled new potatoes, glazed onions and a green salad.

Per portion Energy 337kcal/1407kJ; Protein 30.1g; Carbohydrate 3.8g, of which sugars 3.8g; Fat 20.3g, of which saturates 10.9g; Cholesterol 106mg; Calcium 23mg; Fibre 0.2g; Sodium 95mg.

Braised venison with roasted root vegetables

Farsert rådyrstek med ovnsstekte rotgrønnsaker

Braising is a slightly gentler way of cooking compared to roasting and is ideal if you are unsure of the age of your game. Boning the leg makes it easier for carving and the meat will serve more people than if left on the bone.

1 To make the stuffing, put the dried mushrooms in a bowl and pour over boiling water to cover. Leave to soak for about 15–20 minutes, then drain and chop finely.

2 Preheat the oven to 180°C/350°F/Gas 4. Melt the butter for the stuffing in a pan, add the shallots and sauté for 3 minutes. Add the soaked and chopped mushrooms and the fresh mushrooms and stir over a high heat for 5–7 minutes until tender. Add the juniper berries and chopped marjoram. Season generously with salt and pepper.

3 Put the stuffing inside the leg of venison and either sew or tie with string into a neat parcel. Heat the butter and the oil in a flameproof casserole, add the meat and fry until browned on all sides. Add the carrot, onion, stock, peppercorns and salt to season. Cover the casserole and cook in the oven for about 1½ hours until the meat is tender. If you are using a meat thermometer, the internal temperature of the meat should read 65°C/150°F.

4 Put the prepared vegetables in a shallow ovenproof dish, drizzle over the olive oil, season with salt and pepper and toss together to coat evenly in the oil. Roast in the oven, tossing occasionally, for about 1 hour until all the vegetables are tender.

5 When tender, remove the venison from the casserole and put on a warmed serving dish. Skim off any fat from the cooking juices then strain the juices into a pan to make the sauce. Add the stock and wine, bring to the boil and cook until reduced slightly. Add the cream and reduce further until the sauce is a good pouring consistency.

6 To thicken the sauce, blend the arrowroot with a little cold water to form a smooth paste then add a little of the hot sauce. Stir into the pan and bring to the boil until thickened. Serve the venison with the sauce and root vegetables.

Per portion Energy 459kcal/1919kJ; Protein 44.8g; Carbohydrate 15.2g, of which sugars 10.7g; Fat 25.1g, of which saturates 14.2g; Cholesterol 146mg; Calcium 98mg; Fibre 4.4g; Sodium 195mg.

Serves 6–8

2.5–3kg/5½–6½lb leg of venison, boned

7.5ml/1½ tsp unsalted butter

15ml/1 tbsp vegetable oil

1 carrot, halved lengthways

1 onion, halved

120ml/4fl oz/½ cup beef or venison stock

4–5 black peppercorns

salt

For the stuffing

10g/¼oz dried wild mushrooms

40g/1½oz/3 tbsp unsalted butter

5 shallots, chopped

150g/5oz/2 cups mushrooms, sliced

10ml/2 tsp juniper berries, crushed

5ml/1 tsp chopped fresh marjoram

salt and ground black pepper

For the sauce

475ml/16fl oz/2 cups venison or beef stock

90ml/3½fl oz/scant ½ cup medium white wine

300ml/½ pint/1¼ cups whipping cream

10ml/2 tsp arrowroot (optional)

For the roasted root vegetables

5 onions, quartered

5 carrots, cut into 5cm/2in pieces

3 parsnips, cut into 5cm/2in pieces

1 medium-sized celeriac, cut into 5cm/2in pieces

1 turnip or small swede (rutabaga), cut into 5cm/2in pieces

45ml/3 tbsp olive oil

salt and ground black pepper

Pheasant stuffed with mountain fruits
Farsert orrfuglstek i gryte

The lean, tender meat of the pheasant has always been a great European delicacy. The sweetness of the fruit stuffing here, based on an idea by the Norwegian chef, Arne Brimi, balances the bird's gamey flavour.

1 Cut the prunes into small pieces and put in a bowl. Peel, core and finely dice the apples and add to the prunes. Pour over the lemon juice. Add the berries and rosemary, season and mix together. Fill the bird with the stuffing and truss with string.

2 Melt the butter in a flameproof casserole, and fry the bird until browned. Stand the bird on a small rack in the casserole. Add the wine to cover the rack, and add the rosemary.

3 Cover the casserole and simmer gently for about 1 hour. Insert the point of a sharp knife into the thigh near the body – if the juices are clear, the bird is cooked. Remove the bird and rack from the casserole, put on a warmed serving dish and keep warm.

4 Discard the rosemary sprig and add the sour cream or crème fraîche to the pan juices. Heat the juices, stirring well, until the sauce is a good pouring consistency.

5 Carve the bird, arrange on a dish and garnish with the stuffing and a little sauce. Accompany with the remaining sauce, boiled potatoes and a green vegetable or salad.

Per portion Energy 213kcal/893kJ; Protein 21.3g; Carbohydrate 8.6g, of which sugars 8.6g; Fat 10g, of which saturates 4.5g; Cholesterol 12mg; Calcium 58mg; Fibre 1.7g; Sodium 85mg.

Serves 6–8

1.8–2.25kg/4–5lb pheasant or black grouse, plucked and drawn

15ml/1 tbsp unsalted butter

75ml/2½fl oz/⅓ cup medium white wine

1 rosemary sprig

100ml/3½fl oz/scant ½ cup sour cream or crème fraîche

salt and ground black pepper

For the stuffing

115g/4oz/½ cup pitted prunes

2 apples

juice 1 lemon

115g/4oz/1 cup fresh blueberries or dried cranberries

5ml/1 tsp chopped fresh rosemary

salt and ground black pepper

To serve

boiled new potatoes

a green vegetable or salad

Quail in cream sauce
Rype eller vaktel I fløtesaus

This is a good way of cooking small birds, such as quail, ptarmigan, pigeon and poussin. The slow cooking in cream, butter and the juices from the birds gives them a wonderful flavour, makes the flesh tender and produces a velvety sauce.

1 Melt about 50g/2oz/4 tbsp of the butter in a flameproof casserole dish. When the butter stops frothing, add the parsley and cook until soft. Remove from the heat.

2 Season the inside of each bird with salt and pepper and stuff each one using the parsley,15g/½oz/1 tbsp butter and a lump of sugar. Return the casserole dish to the heat, add the remaining butter and heat until melted. Add the birds and fry until browned on all sides. Season the birds with salt and pepper.

3 Add a little cream to the dish, cover, leaving a gap for steam to escape, and simmer very gently, adding a little more cream from time to time, until the flesh almost falls off the bone. The cooking time will depend on the birds' size. The quail will take 30–40 minutes, the ptarmigan or pigeons about 1½ hours and the poussin about 1 hour 15 minutes. Remove the birds from the dish and place on a warmed serving dish.

4 Lightly whip the remaining cream and add to the cooking juices. Heat gently and serve the sauce with the birds. Accompany with boiled new potatoes and green beans.

Per portion Energy 1033kcal/4264kJ; Protein 30.8g; Carbohydrate 1.6g, of which sugars 1.6g; Fat 100.4g, of which saturates 54.4g; Cholesterol 223mg; Calcium 64mg; Fibre 0g; Sodium 468mg.

Serves 4

about 225g/8oz/1 cup butter

1 large bunch fresh parsley

6–8 quail, 2 ptarmigan, 4 pigeon or 2–4 poussin, depending on size

2–8 sugar lumps

300ml/½ pint/1¼ cups double (heavy) cream

salt and ground black pepper

To serve

boiled new potatoes

green beans

Roast hare with lingonberries
Harestek med tyttebær

Fresh hare is available throughout the shooting season in Norway, which runs from August until the end of February. A young hare is the best choice as it is the most tender. All hares have a delicious gamey flavour but as they get older, the flesh becomes tougher. Although a young hare does not need to be marinated, doing this does add more flavour.

Serves 4–6

1 hare (jack rabbit), skinned and jointed into serving pieces

40g/1½oz/3 tbsp butter

45–60ml/3–4 tbsp Dijon mustard

30–45ml/2–3 tbsp lingonberries or crushed cranberries

475ml/16fl oz/2 cups chicken stock

salt and ground black pepper

For the marinade

1 bottle red wine or 350ml/12fl oz/1½ cups wine vinegar

90ml/6 tbsp olive oil

1 small onion, sliced

15ml/1 tbsp black peppercorns

1 bay leaf

1 thyme sprig

For the sauce

5ml/1 tsp potato flour

15ml/1 tbsp water

45ml/3 tbsp double (heavy) cream

30ml/2 tbsp port (optional)

15ml/1 tbsp lingonberries or crushed cranberries

salt and ground black pepper

1 To make the marinade, put the wine or vinegar, olive oil, onion, peppercorns, bay leaf and thyme in a large bowl. Remove the whitish-blue membrane and any fine skin on the hare. Add the joints to the marinade and leave to marinate at room temperature for 2–3 hours. Remove the joints from the marinade and drain on kitchen paper.

2 Preheat the oven to 180°C/350°F/Gas 4. Melt the butter. Season the joints with salt and pepper and brush with the mustard. Put only the leg joints in a roasting pan and baste with some of the melted butter. Add the lingonberries or crushed cranberries.

3 Roast the joints in the oven for 10 minutes. Add the back pieces to the pan, baste with melted butter and continue roasting for about 1 hour until tender. Continue basting with the butter every 10 minutes and when all the butter has been used, baste with the stock. When the hare is cooked, transfer the pieces to a warmed serving dish and keep warm.

4 Strain the juices into a pan and return to the boil. In a small bowl, blend the potato flour with the water to form a smooth paste then add a little of the hot juices. Stir into the pan and heat but do not boil, stirring all the time until thickened. Check the seasoning, adding salt and pepper only if necessary. Add the cream, port, if using, and the berries and serve the sauce with the hare.

Per portion Energy 274kcal/1140kJ; Protein 22.6g; Carbohydrate 2g, of which sugars 1.1g; Fat 19.6g, of which saturates 6.5g; Cholesterol 25mg; Calcium 28mg; Fibre 0.2g; Sodium 293mg.

Desserts

Purées, baked fruit and whipped cream

Norwegians love their desserts. Fresh or cooked fruit is the everyday pudding, and also appears on the breakfast table. As an alternative to fresh fruit, dried fruit such as apricots or prunes can be cooked, with the juices usually thickened with a little potato flour or arrowroot. Apples are very popular – apple purée can be enjoyed on its own, or try Peasant Girls in a Veil, traditional in the autumn as soon as cooking apples are ripe; it is typically served after the lamb casserole fårikål. Sweet soups are made with berries, rosehips or any other fruit and are served both hot and cold – a traditional favourite is rhubarb soup, its distinctive colour heralds the approach of summer.

Rice is another commonly used Norwegian ingredient. A rice pudding containing a single almond is served at the Christmas feast, usually at the start of the celebrations, and whoever gets the almond in their portion has luck throughout the coming year. Another dish that uses creamed rice mixed with fruit, particularly orange, makes the most delicious dessert, Ris à la Malta. Norwegians are also passionate about dairy products. Sour cream porridge, made with full fat (whole) milk and garnished with cinnamon, is produced for all special occasions. One of the most loved desserts is Caramel Pudding, edged with chopped blanched almonds.

Every Norwegian cook has their favourite layer cake. Great trouble is taken to decorate these, usually involving beautifully arranged berries on whipped cream. Waffles and pancakes are also essential features of the dessert table.

Norwegians often leave the clutter of the table and produce dessert with coffee, elegantly handed round on small plates in a sitting area – a stylish end to any meal.

Serves 12

25g/1oz/2 tbsp butter

3 eggs

115g/4oz/1 cup plain white (all-purpose) flour

350ml/12fl oz/1½ cups milk

pinch of salt

pinch of ground cinnamon

vegetable oil, for shallow frying

jam or sugar and cinnamon, or fresh fruit berries, such as raspberries, sour cream or whipped cream and icing (confectioners') sugar, to serve

Norwegian pancakes
Pannekaker

Norwegian pancakes are closely related to French crêpes. They are served with sugar and cinnamon for breakfast, or for dessert filled with lingonberries or strawberries and cream, or a spoonful of blueberry jelly and sour cream.

1 Melt the butter. Put the eggs in a bowl and beat lightly together, then sift in the flour. Add the milk, melted butter, salt and cinnamon and mix together to form a smooth, thin batter. Alternatively, this can be done in a food processor. Leave to rest for 30 minutes to an hour until the flour is absorbed into the mixture.

2 Heat a frying pan measuring about 18cm/7in. Add a little oil and when hot, add enough batter to swirl around the base of the pan in a thin layer. Cook until golden brown then slip a metal spatula underneath and turn over or toss. Cook briefly on the other side until a spotted brown colour, then remove from the pan and repeat the process with the remaining batter.

3 To serve the pancakes, spread a line of butter across the centre of the pancake, add jam or sugar and cinnamon. Alternatively, add fresh berries and sour cream or whipped cream, roll up or fold over the pancake and dust with icing sugar.

Per portion Energy 105kcal/438kJ; Protein 3.5g; Carbohydrate 8.8g, of which sugars 1.5g; Fat 6.5g, of which saturates 2.1g; Cholesterol 54mg; Calcium 56mg; Fibre 0.3g; Sodium 43mg.

Cook's tip When turning a pancake over, don't try to flip it in the pan too soon. The secret is to make sure it is cooked before turning.

Rice pudding with oranges
Ris à la Malta

This pudding is very different from the standard English rice pudding, as it has a depth and sophistication that lift it into a class of its own. The serving suggestion is small pieces of orange segments folded into the cooked rice.

1 Bring the water to the boil then slowly add the rice so that the water continues to boil. Reduce the heat and simmer for 10–15 minutes until the water is absorbed.

2 Add the milk to the rice, return to the boil then simmer for 30–40 minutes until the rice is cooked. Season with the salt and sweeten to taste with the sugar. Add the vanilla extract or cinnamon. Turn into a bowl and leave to cool.

3 Segment the oranges by cutting off the top and bottom with a small sharp knife. Cut down around the orange, removing the peel and pith. Hold the orange in one hand and slip the blade of the knife between each segment and its membrane to release it and lift out the segment. Cut each segment into three pieces.

4 Whisk the cream until it just holds its shape then fold into the rice. Fold in the orange pieces and serve hot.

Per portion Energy 322kcal/1345kJ; Protein 11.5g; Carbohydrate 46.5g, of which sugars 16.6g; Fat 10g, of which saturates 6.3g; Cholesterol 35mg; Calcium 312mg; Fibre 0.8g; Sodium 109mg.

Serves 4

400ml/14fl oz/1⅔ cups water

150g/5oz/¾ cup short grain rice

1 litre/1¾ pints/4 cups full fat (whole) milk

5ml/1 tsp salt

sugar, to taste

5ml/1 tsp vanilla extract or 5ml/1 tsp ground cinnamon

2–3 fresh oranges

Variation Alternatively, serve the rice pudding with 115g/4oz raspberries, stewed fruit, jam or a fruit sauce.

Honey and ginger baked apples
Stekte epler med vaniljsaus

Norway is the most northern country to grow apples and most are cultivated in the Hardanger valley in the south. The short summers are compensated for by the length of the days and the Gulf Stream softens the effect of the northerly latitude. There are many Norwegian variations on baked apples. This recipe has its roots in one by Andreas Viestad, the Norwegian food writer and chef.

1 To make the vanilla sauce, put the cream and vanilla pod in a pan and heat gently to just below boiling point. Remove from the heat and leave to infuse for 10 minutes. Remove the vanilla pod.

2 Put the egg yolks and sugar in a bowl and whisk them together until pale and thick, then slowly pour in the cream in a steady stream, whisking all the time. Return the pan to the heat and heat very gently until the cream is thick enough to coat the back of a wooden spoon. (If you draw a finger horizontally across the back of the spoon, the sauce should be thick enough not to run down through the channel.) Remove from the heat and leave to cool. Either stir from time to time or cover to prevent a skin forming.

3 Preheat the oven to 160°C/325°F Gas 3. Remove the cores from the apples leaving the stalk end intact, but remove the actual stalk. Fill each cavity with 2.5ml/$^1/_2$ tbsp chopped ginger and 15ml/1 tbsp honey.

4 Place the apples in an ovenproof dish, with the open end uppermost, and top each one with a knob of butter. Pour in the wine and bake in the oven, basting frequently with the cooking juices, for about 45 minutes, until the apples are tender.

5 Serve the apples with the vanilla sauce, sour cream or double cream.

Serves 4

4 eating apples, such as Cox's Orange Pippin or Golden Delicious

30ml/2 tbsp finely chopped fresh root ginger

60ml/4 tbsp honey

25g/1oz/2 tbsp unsalted butter

60ml/4 tbsp medium white wine

vanilla sauce, sour cream or double (heavy) cream, to serve

For the vanilla sauce

300ml/$^1/_2$ pint/1$^1/_4$ cups single (light) cream

1 vanilla pod (bean), split lengthways

2 egg yolks

30ml/2 tbsp caster (superfine) sugar

Cook's tips

• If the sauce looks as though it may overheat, plunge the base of the pan into a bowl of cold water. This will cool the contents and prevent it curdling. Should the sauce curdle, pour it into a food processor and blend until smooth.
• A final touch of luxury is to fold a little whipped cream into the sauce just before serving.

Per portion Energy 331kcal/1381kJ; Protein 4.3g; Carbohydrate 27.8g, of which sugars 27.8g; Fat 22.3g, of which saturates 13.2g; Cholesterol 155mg; Calcium 89mg; Fibre 1.2g; Sodium 68mg.

Rhubarb soup
Rabarbrasuppe

Traditionally, everyone in Norway had a rhubarb patch, usually near the barn. Rhubarb is a plant that produces ample fruit without taking up much land, which is important when fertile land is limited. Although Norwegians are fond of savoury fruit soups, this is a dessert, made with the first picked rhubarb, and was a traditional treat after the long winter.

1 In a pan, bring the water to the boil. Add the rhubarb and cinnamon stick and simmer for about 5 minutes, until the rhubarb is tender. Remove the cinnamon stick and add sugar to taste.

2 Put the potato flour in a small bowl, add a little water and blend together to form a smooth paste. Add to the rhubarb and heat, stirring all the time, until thickened and clear, but do not bring to the boil. Remove from the heat and add the salt.

3 Serve the soup hot or cold and garnish each bowl with a spoonful of crème fraîche or sour cream.

Per portion Energy 179kcal/765kJ; Protein 1.4g; Carbohydrate 46g, of which sugars 40.2g; Fat 0.2g, of which saturates 0g; Cholesterol 0mg; Calcium 137mg; Fibre 1.8g; Sodium 9mg.

Serves 4

1.2 litre/2 pints/5 cups water

500g/1¼lb rhubarb, cut into small lengths

1 cinnamon stick (optional)

150g/5oz/¾ cup sugar

25g/1oz potato flour

pinch of salt

crème fraîche or sour cream, to serve

Variations
• Add strawberries to the soup, which combine beautifully with the rhubarb.
• Instead of the cinnamon stick, add the grated rind of 1 orange.

Serves 4

1kg/2¼lb cooking apples

45ml/3 tbsp water

sugar, to taste

115g/4oz/½ cup butter

65g/2½oz/1¼ cups fresh breadcrumbs

45ml/3 tbsp sugar

350ml/12fl oz/1½ cups whipping cream

50g/2oz/½ cup toasted almonds, roughly chopped, to decorate

Cook's tip Do not prepare the dish too far ahead of serving or the breadcrumbs will lose their crispness.

Peasant girls in a veil
Tilslørte Bondepiker

This cooking apple recipe is probably the most famous Norwegian dessert and is traditional in all the Scandinavian countries. The Norwegian version uses cream in generous layers between the apple sauce and the crumbs. The final layer of cream is the veil in the recipe title.

1 Peel, core and cut the apples into small pieces. Simmer in a pan with the water for 10–15 minutes until the apples are soft. Leave to cool and add sugar to taste.

2 Melt the butter in a frying pan and when hot, add the breadcrumbs and sugar and fry, stirring frequently, until the breadcrumbs are golden brown. Remove from the heat and leave to cool. (The crumbs will become crisper as they cool.)

3 Whisk the cream until it holds its shape. Layer the apples, cream and breadcrumbs in glass serving dishes, ending with a layer of cream. Sprinkle with the chopped almonds.

Per portion Energy 813kcal/3380kJ; Protein 7.3g; Carbohydrate 50g, of which sugars 37.5g; Fat 66.4g, of which saturates 37.6g; Cholesterol 153mg; Calcium 123mg; Fibre 5.3g; Sodium 327mg.

Serves 4

115g/4oz/½ cup plus 30ml/2 tbsp sugar

30ml/2 tbsp hot water

3 large eggs

3 large egg yolks

600ml/1 pint/2½ cups full fat milk, or a mixture of milk and single (light) cream

1 vanilla pod (bean), split lengthways

chopped blanched almonds, to decorate

Caramel pudding
Karamellpudding

Every country home used to have at least one cow and milk is a staple of the country's diet. This simple but delicious pudding is a great Norwegian favourite.

1 Preheat the oven to 160°C/325°F/Gas 3. For the caramel, put the sugar in a pan over a medium heat until golden. Add the hot water carefully. Stir together. Pour the caramel into a round, 1 litre/1¾ pint ovenproof dish and swirl the caramel around to coat the bottom and a little way up the sides. It will set instantly.

2 Mix the eggs and egg yolks and the remaining sugar in a bowl (don't whisk). Using the caramel pan, heat the milk with the split vanilla pod to just below boiling.

3 Remove the vanilla pod from the milk and whisk the milk into the egg and sugar. Strain through a sieve (strainer) into the caramel dish. Place in a roasting pan and fill with cold water to come about three-quarters of the way up the sides.

4 Bake the custard for 45 minutes to 1 hour. Leave until cool, then chill for 2–3 hours. Having run a knife around the edge, place a serving dish over the top of the custard and invert the caramel on to the dish. Decorate with chopped almonds.

Per portion Energy 296kcal/1248kJ; Protein 13.1g; Carbohydrate 37.1g, of which sugars 37.1g; Fat 11.8g, of which saturates 4.2g; Cholesterol 337mg; Calcium 239mg; Fibre 0g; Sodium 136mg.

Cook's tip The creamy texture of the custard depends on slow cooking. Filling the roasting pan with cold water coming three-quarters of the way up the sides of the caramel dish helps to filter the heat.

Blueberry ice cream parfait
Blåbæris

Autumn in Norway is the season for hunting wild berries. Wild bilberries are related to the larger, cultivated blueberry, and they are the perfect fruit to use for this ice cream because they have more flavour than the cultivated variety. However, blueberries still give a great flavour. This ice cream can also be made with almost any soft berry, such as raspberries, blackberries or blackcurrants.

1 Put the egg yolks and half the sugar in a bowl and whisk together until pale and thick. Beat in about three-quarters of the blueberries and reserve the remainder for decorating. Blend in the berries so that they burst and spread their colour.

2 Whisk the egg whites until they stand in soft peaks, then whisk in the remaining sugar. Fold into the blueberry mixture. Whisk the cream with the aquavit, if using, until it just holds its shape, and fold into the blueberry mixture. Transfer to a mould or freezer container and freeze for 6–8 hours until firm.

3 Unless the berries were very juicy, it should be possible to serve the ice cream parfait straight from the freezer. If the berries produced a lot of juice, put the parfait in the refrigerator for about 20 minutes to soften slightly before required. To serve, dip the mould briefly in hot water before turning out and decorate with the reserved blueberries.

Per portion Energy 536kcal/2228kJ; Protein 4.9g; Carbohydrate 34.6g, of which sugars 34.6g; Fat 43.1g, of which saturates 25.8g; Cholesterol 198mg; Calcium 96mg; Fibre 1.8g; Sodium 55mg.

Serves 4

2 large eggs, separated

115g/4oz/1 cup icing (confectioners') sugar

200g/7oz/1¾ cup blueberries

300ml/½ pint/1¼ cups double (heavy) cream

30ml/2 tbsp aquavit (optional)

Variation This basic recipe can be used with any number of different flavourings, such as the grated rind of 1 orange, 30ml/2 tbsp chopped stem ginger or 30ml/2 tbsp raisins and 30ml/2 tbsp rum.

Serves 6–8

115g/4oz/1 cup plain (all-purpose) flour

5ml/1 tsp baking powder

300g/11oz/1½ cups caster (superfine) sugar

90g/3½oz/scant ½ cup unsalted butter

4 eggs, separated

45–60ml/3–4 tbsp full fat (whole) milk

60ml/4 tbsp roughly chopped almonds

For the vanilla cream

50g/2oz/¼ cup vanilla sugar or 50g/2oz/¼ cup caster (superfine) sugar and 5ml/1 tsp vanilla extract

25g/1oz/2 tbsp plain (all-purpose) flour

7.5ml/1½ tsp cornflour

1 large egg, beaten

300ml/½ pint/1¼ cups full fat (whole) milk

25g/1oz/2 tbsp butter

300ml/½ pint/1¼ cups whipping cream

Cook's tip The cake can be baked in a Swiss roll tin (jelly roll pan) instead of two sandwich tins, and then cut in half before being sandwiched together with the vanilla cream.

Kvaefjord cake with vanilla cream
Kvæfjordkake med vaniljekrem

This is a superb example of the Norwegian's love of elaborate gâteaux and shows their skill in devising delicious variations. While you can buy packets of vanilla cream, the classic recipe here produces a more delicious result. The cake provides a perfect end to a meal, or can just be served with coffee.

1 Put the vanilla sugar or sugar and vanilla extract, flour, cornflour and egg in a bowl and blend together. Heat the milk in a pan to just below boiling point, then gradually stir into the flour mixture. Rinse out the pan then return the mixture to the pan and heat gently, stirring all the time, until the mixture comes to the boil. Remove from the heat and stir in the butter.

2 Put the mixture in a bowl and cover with clear film (plastic wrap) to prevent skin from forming. Cool. Whisk the cream until it holds its shape and fold into the custard.

3 Preheat the oven to 180°C/350°F/Gas 4. Line the base of two 19cm/7½in sandwich tins (layer cake pans) with baking parchment. Sift the flour and baking powder together. Put 100g/4oz/½ cup of the sugar and the butter in a bowl and whisk together until pale and fluffy. Add the egg yolks, one at a time, beating well after each addition. Add the sifted flour alternately with the milk. Spread the mixture into the tins.

4 Whisk the egg whites until they strand in soft peaks then whisk in the remaining 200g/7oz/1 cup sugar, a tablespoonful at a time, until the mixture stands in glossy peaks. Spread over the cake mixture in each tin. Sprinkle with chopped almonds.

5 Bake the cakes in an oven for 20–30 minutes until the cakes are slightly risen, the meringue slightly crisp and the almonds toasted. Leave to cool in the tins.

6 When the cakes are cold, remove from the tins and place one cake on a serving plate. Cover with the vanilla cream then place the second cake on top and serve.

Per portion Energy 605kcal/2526kJ; Protein 8.9g; Carbohydrate 63.8g, of which sugars 49.4g; Fat 36.7g, of which saturates 19.8g; Cholesterol 173mg; Calcium 156mg; Fibre 1.1g; Sodium 162mg.

Cream layer cake
Bløtkake

This is the Norwegian celebration cake, suitable for any special occasion but especially good on the 17th May, the Norwegian national day, when the national constitution was adopted. The possibilities for the presentation of the basic cake are numerous and cooks pride themselves on their elaborate arrangements of fruit and whipped cream.

1 Preheat the oven to160°C/325°F/Gas 3. Line a 23cm/9in round cake tin (pan) with baking parchment. Sift the flour, potato flour, if using, and baking powder together. Put the eggs and sugar in a bowl and whisk until pale and the mixture will form ribbons on the surface if lifted and allowed to fall back into the bowl. Fold in the sifted flour until well combined. Turn the mixture into the prepared tin.

2 Bake the cake in the oven for about 40 minutes until firm to the touch and beginning to come away from the sides of the tin. Leave in the tin for 5 minutes, then carefully turn out on to a wire rack to cool.

3 Cut the cooled cake horizontally into three rounds. Place the top round, upside down, on to a serving plate. Sprinkle with peach juice from the can. Spread with raspberry jam, then add a layer of peaches and a layer of vanilla cream. Put the middle cake round on top and repeat the layers, adding a final layer of peaches and vanilla cream. Finally add the bottom round of cake, upside down to give a perfectly flat top layer, and sprinkle with juice but omit the jam, peaches and vanilla cream.

4 Whisk the cream and the sugar together until the cream just holds its shape. Use the cream to cover the top and sides of the cake reserving a little, if you wish, to pipe on top. Arrange the fresh fruit berries decoratively on top. Pipe the reserved cream, if you wish, around and between the different groups of berries. Alternatively, if fresh berries are not available, decorate with more canned peaches.

Serves 6–8

115g/4oz/1 cup plain (all-purpose) flour, to include 15ml/1 tbsp potato flour (optional)

5ml/1 tsp baking powder

4 large eggs

90g/3½oz/½ cup caster (superfine) sugar

For the filling

2 x 400g/14oz/2½ cups sliced peaches

raspberry jam

1 quantity vanilla cream (see page 106)

300ml/½ pint/1¼ cups double (heavy) cream

5ml/1 tsp sugar

3 varieties fresh fruit berries, such as raspberries, strawberries, bilberries or blueberries, or canned peaches

Per portion Energy 363kcal/1513kJ; Protein 5.7g; Carbohydrate 35.2g, of which sugars 24.3g; Fat 23.1g, of which saturates 13.3g; Cholesterol 147mg; Calcium 64mg; Fibre 1.3g; Sodium 57mg.

Cook's tips
• Traditionally, Norwegians like to add sugar to their cream before whipping it.
• Avoid moving the cake rounds after they have been sprinkled with juice as they could fall apart. Instead, have them in place on the serving dish before sprinkling with juice.

Baking

Bread, pastries, cookies, and cakes

In Norway the traditional flour was always barley, a highly nutritious grain. Because it does not contain gluten, for baking it is best suited to hardbreads. When baking yeast-raised breads and rolls, barley flour is mixed with wheat flour. Oats were rarely used in baking, but rye played an important part.

Hardbreads have several advantages. They do not require a raising agent, so can be baked on a griddle or over an open fire, dispensing with the need for an oven. They can also be made in large quantities and stored for the winter pantry.

Lefse is a traditional Norwegian soft bread that keeps well, making it popular among fishermen. Lofoten islanders used to store the bread in storage chests and resoften it before eating by wrapping it in a damp towel. There are many lefse recipes – one popular version uses cooked and mashed potato mixed with flour. Traditional rolling pins were carved in a knotted pattern, helping to produce a thin result.

The introduction of stoves with ovens resulted in an impressive range of yeast-raised breads, many of them containing spices, dried fruits and custards that result in mouthwatering yeast buns, wreaths and pastries.

The Norwegian housewife prided herself on producing a variety of baked goods whenever a visitor called, always accompanied by coffee. Various irons were used for cooking batter cookies, cones and wafers, some baked on griddles and others deep fried. Sometimes pastries or a nut cake would be available, but always biscuits or cookies, with seven different kinds traditionally baked at Christmas. And the famous Norwegian celebration cake, Kransekake, made with staggered-sized rings of almond paste, is a prerequisite for any wedding.

Vanilla Christmas biscuits
Vaniljehjerter

These heart-shaped treats are a perfect choice for a Christmas bake-in. They are not only ideal with a cup of tea or coffee but can accompany a dessert such as fruit salad. A little box of them wrapped with a big red bow also makes a delightful present.

1 Sift the flour and baking powder together. Put the butter and sugar in a large bowl and beat together until light and fluffy. Add the egg and vanilla extract, then add the milk, alternating it with the sifted flour. Mix together, then knead the dough lightly. Chill in the refrigerator for 30 minutes.

2 Preheat the oven to 180°C/350°F/Gas 4. Butter a large baking tray. On a lightly floured surface, roll out the dough to 1cm/½in thickness. Using a heart-shaped cutter, cut out hearts and place on the prepared baking tray. Bring the pastry trimmings together, knead lightly, roll and cut out more hearts.

3 Bake the biscuits (cookies) for about 10 minutes until lightly golden brown. Leave on the tray for 2–3 minutes, then transfer to a wire rack and leave to cool.

Per biscuit Energy 100kcal/420kJ; Protein 1.4g; Carbohydrate 11.9g, of which sugars 4.8g; Fat 5.6g, of which saturates 3.4g; Cholesterol 22mg; Calcium 24mg; Fibre 0.3g; Sodium 43mg.

Makes about 24

225g/8oz/2 cups plain (all-purpose) flour

5ml/1 tsp baking powder

150g/5oz/10 tbsp butter, at room temperature

90g/3½ oz/½ cup caster (superfine) sugar

1 egg, lightly beaten

7.5ml/1½ tsp vanilla extract

120ml/4fl oz/½ cup milk

Cook's tip A pretty finish could be provided by brushing the hearts with lightly beaten egg white and sprinkling with caster sugar before baking.

Makes about 48

2 hard-boiled eggs, yolks only

2 eggs, separated

225g/8oz/1 generous cup sugar

475g/1lb/4½ cups plain (all-purpose) flour

350g/12oz/1½ cups butter, softened

coarse sugar, for coating

Berlin wreath biscuits
Berlinerkranser

These are traditional favourites for enjoying at Christmas. They are unusual in that cooked egg yolk is used in addition to raw eggs and the mixture produces a very appealing texture.

1 Put the hard-boiled egg yolks and fresh egg yolks in a bowl and mash together. Beat in the sugar, a little at a time. Add the flour alternately with the softened butter, mixing well to make a stiff dough. Wrap the dough in clear film (plastic wrap) and put in the refrigerator for 2–3 hours.

2 Line a baking tray with baking parchment. On a lightly floured surface, using your hands, roll out pieces of the dough into strips the thickness of a pencil. Cut into 10–13cm/4–5in lengths, then form into small wreaths by making a round loop and placing one end over the other. Place on the prepared baking tray and chill in the refrigerator for 30 minutes.

3 Preheat the oven to 190°C/375°F/Gas 5. Lightly beat the egg white, brush over each wreath then dip into coarse sugar. Return to the baking tray and bake in the oven for 10–12 minutes until very light brown. Leave on the baking tray for 2–3 minutes, then transfer to a wire rack and leave to cool. Store the biscuits (cookies) in an airtight tin.

Per biscuit Energy 107kcal/447kJ; Protein 1.1g; Carbohydrate 12.1g, of which sugars 4.5g; Fat 6.4g, of which saturates 3.9g; Cholesterol 24mg; Calcium 18mg; Fibre 0.3g; Sodium 45mg.

Cook's tip The wreaths spread during cooking so make sure that the loops are large enough not to close up during baking. Chilling the wreaths in the refrigerator before cooking helps to stop the dough spreading too much.

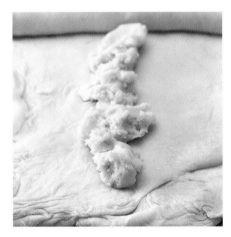

Makes 1 wreath

300ml/½ pint/1¼ cups milk

1 packet dried yeast

1 egg plus 1 egg yolk

30ml/2 tbsp sugar

450g/1lb/4 cups plain (all purpose) flour

225g/8oz/1 cup butter, chilled

For the filling

115g/4oz/1 cup ground almonds

115g/4oz/1 cup icing (confectioners') sugar

2 egg whites, lightly beaten

To glaze

1 egg yolk

15ml/1 tbsp milk

coarse sugar

Birthday wreath
Fødselsdagskringle

In Norway, birthdays begin with a coffee tray taken up to the bedroom and this celebration wreath often accompanies the coffee. It is best eaten on the day it is baked, but this is easily achieved as the wreath is allowed to rise overnight and then presented in the early morning, fresh from the oven.

1 Line a baking tray with baking parchment. To make the filling, put the ground almonds and the icing sugar in a bowl and then add enough egg white to make a soft marzipan.

2 In a pan, bring the milk to just below boiling point. Pour the milk into a large bowl and leave until lukewarm. Sprinkle in the dried yeast and leave for 15 minutes until frothy.

3 Add the egg and egg yolk, sugar and flour to the mixture and mix together to make a stiff dough that leaves the sides of the bowl clean.

4 On a lightly floured surface, roll out the dough into a rectangle, three times as long as it is wide. Cut the cold butter into thin slices and use to cover the bottom two-thirds of the dough. Fold the top third over the middle and then turn the folded two-thirds over on to the bottom third. Turn the dough so that the folded edges are at the sides and roll out again to the same size rectangle. Fold again into three and roll out into a rectangle measuring 20 x 75cm/8 x 30in.

5 Spread the filling down the centre of the long length of the dough, then fold each side of the dough to the middle, over the filling, making a secure tube.

6 Place the dough and filling on the prepared baking tray and bend the dough into a wreath, tucking one end underneath a longer end, twisting this longer, upper end so that it sits in the middle of the circle.

7 Cover the wreath loosely with clear film (plastic wrap) and put in the refrigerator or a very cool place to rise overnight.

8 Preheat the oven to 230°C/450°F/Gas 8. Meanwhile, take the wreath out of the refrigerator or pantry and allow to stand at room temperature.

9 In a small bowl, beat together the egg yolk and milk and brush over the wreath. Sprinkle coarse sugar over the top.

10 Place the wreath in the oven and reduce the heat to 220°C/425°F/Gas 7. Bake for about 20 minutes until golden brown. Leave to cool on a wire rack.

Per wreath Energy 4779kcal/20001kJ; Protein 93.7g; Carbohydrate 524.6g, of which sugars 178.6g; Fat 271.1g, of which saturates 129.5g; Cholesterol 889mg; Calcium 1438mg; Fibre 22.5g; Sodium 1731mg.

Makes about 35

1kg/2¼lb potatoes

40g/1½oz/3 tbsp butter

120ml/4fl oz/½ cup single (light) cream

450–600g/1–1⅓lb/4–5 cups plain (all-purpose) flour

salt

Thin potato bread
Lefse

A traditional Norwegian bread, the many types of lefse are all are very thin, slightly soft breads. They can be eaten buttered and sprinkled with sugar or served with honey, lingonberry or cloudberry jam. Lefse can also be wrapped around a hotdog or filled with meat or fish and a salad.

1 Peel and cut the potatoes. Bring to the boil in a pan of salted water and simmer for about 20 minutes until tender. Drain and put through a ricer or a sieve (strainer) into a large bowl. Add the butter, cream and 5ml/1 tsp salt and beat together. Leave to cool.

2 When the potatoes are cool, add enough flour to form a firm dough. On a lightly floured surface, knead until smooth. Divide the dough into pieces about the size of a large egg, roll into balls and put on a baking tray. Chill in the refrigerator for 30 minutes.

3 On a floured surface, roll out each ball of dough very thinly. Heat a large ungreased frying pan or griddle and cook the breads over a medium heat, one at a time, until brown spots appear on the surface. Turn and cook the second side. Put the breads between two dish towels to stop them from drying out. Serve immediately.

Per portion Energy 71kcal/301kJ; Protein 1.8g; Carbohydrate 14.7g, of which sugars 0.6g; Fat 1g, of which saturates 0.5g; Cholesterol 2mg; Calcium 23mg; Fibre 0.7g; Sodium 5mg.

Cardamom buns
Juleboller

Norwegian children have been brought up on these buns. This is an example of Norway's fondness for the very individual flavour of cardamom.

1 Line a baking tray with baking parchment. Melt the butter and leave until lukewarm. Bring the milk to just below boiling point. Pour into a jug (pitcher) and leave until warm. Sprinkle in the yeast and the 2.5ml/½ tsp sugar and leave for 15 minutes until frothy.

2 Put the flour in a large bowl, add the remaining sugar, salt and crushed cardamom seeds and mix well together. Add the milk mixture and the melted butter to the flour mixture and mix together to make a stiff dough that leaves the sides of the bowl clean.

3 Knead the dough on a floured surface until it feels firm and elastic. Put the dough in a bowl, cover with a damp dish towel and leave in a warm place to double in size. Turn the dough on to a lightly floured surface, knock down and knead for 2–3 minutes. Divide the dough into 24 equal pieces and shape each one into a ball. Put on the baking tray and leave to rise for about 20 minutes until nearly doubled in size.

4 Preheat the oven to 230°C/450°F/Gas 8. Brush the buns lightly with beaten egg to glaze and bake in the oven for about 8 minutes until golden brown.

Makes 24

115g/4oz/½ cup butter

350ml/12fl oz/1½ cups milk

1 packet dried yeast

75g/3oz/6 tbsp caster (superfine) sugar, plus 2.5ml/½ tsp caster sugar

450g/1lb/4 cups strong white bread flour

2.5ml/½ tsp salt

10ml/2 tsp cardamom seeds, well crushed

beaten egg, to glaze

Cook's tip In Norway, on the first Sunday in Lent, the buns are cut in half, filled with whipped cream and the tops covered in sifted icing (confectioner's) sugar to be served as a dessert.

Per bun Energy 119kcal/499kJ; Protein 2.3g; Carbohydrate 18.6g, of which sugars 4.3g; Fat 4.4g, of which saturates 2.7g; Cholesterol 11mg; Calcium 46mg; Fibre 0.6g; Sodium 36mg.

Makes 2 loaves

250ml/8fl oz/1 cup milk

115g/4oz/½ cup butter

120ml/4fl oz/½ cup warm water

90g/3½oz/½ cup caster (superfine) sugar, plus 5ml/1 tsp

2 packets dried yeast

1 egg, lightly beaten

5ml/½ tsp salt

5ml/½ tsp cardamom seeds, crushed

500g/1¼lb/5 cups strong white bread flour

115g/4oz/½ cup candied peel, chopped

150g/5oz/1 cup raisins

beaten egg, to glaze (optional)

To finish

melted butter or icing (confectioners') sugar

glacé (candied) cherries

nuts, such as almonds or mixed chopped nuts

Cook's tip If icing (confectioner's) sugar is dusted on the loaves as soon as they come out of the oven, it partially melts and helps the cherries and nuts to stick to the bread.

Christmas bread
Julekake

This is a rich, dried fruit bread, which is traditionally served during the Christmas celebration. It is often made and given as a gift, wrapped in polythene and tied with a big red bow.

1 Grease two 450g/1lb loaf tins (pans) or a large baking tray. In a pan, bring the milk to just below boiling point. Add the butter and stir until melted. Pour into a large bowl and leave until lukewarm. Put the water and the 5ml/1 tsp sugar in a small bowl, sprinkle in the yeast and leave in a warm place for 15 minutes until frothy.

2 Add the egg to the milk mixture then add the yeast mixture, remaining sugar, salt and cardamom seeds. Add half the flour and beat the mixture thoroughly. Dust the fruit generously with flour and add to the mixture with sufficient flour to make a stiff dough that leaves the sides of the bowl clean.

3 Turn the dough on to a lightly floured surface and knead well until the dough feels firm and elastic. Put the dough in a bowl, cover with a damp dish towel and leave in a warm place to rise until doubled in size.

4 Turn the risen dough on to a lightly floured surface, knock down and knead again for 2–3 minutes. Shape the dough into two loaves and place in the prepared tins or shape into rounds and put on the baking tray. Leave to rise again until nearly doubled in size.

5 Preheat the oven to 180°C/350°F/Gas 4. If you wish, brush the loaves with beaten egg to glaze. Bake in the oven for 30–40 minutes until golden brown and the loaves sound hollow when knocked on the bottom.

6 Brush the cooked loaves with melted butter or dust with icing sugar and decorate with glacé cherries and nuts. Leave to cool on a wire rack.

Per loaf Energy 1889kcal/7972kJ; Protein 33.2g; Carbohydrate 333.5g, of which sugars 143g; Fat 56.3g, of which saturates 32.6g; Cholesterol 225mg; Calcium 658mg; Fibre 12g; Sodium 654mg.

Tosca cake
Toscakake

Almonds are very popular throughout Scandinavia and tosca cake uses them in a wonderful, irresistible topping. The cake is a guaranteed success on any coffee or tea table. The following recipe is my mother's, and it has more topping than the more classic version. If you prefer, use half the amount of topping for a lighter effect.

1 Preheat the oven to 160°C/325°F/Gas 3. Butter and line the base and sides of 20cm/8in round cake tin (pan) with baking parchment. Melt the butter and leave to cool. Sift together the flour, baking powder and salt.

2 In a large bowl, whisk the eggs until thick and pale and then gradually whisk in the sugar until the mixture falls in a thick ribbon. Fold in the flour mixture and the cooled butter.

3 Pour the mixture into the prepared tin and tap lightly on a work surface to settle the mixture. Bake the cake in the oven for 30 minutes, or until just before the cake is cooked, when it is almost firm to the touch but needs another few minutes not to sink if removed from the heat.

4 Leave the cake in the oven and prepare the topping. Place the butter, almonds, sugar, flour and cream or milk in a pan and heat gently, stirring, until the butter has melted, then continue heating the mixture until it just reaches boiling point.

5 Preheat the grill (broiler) to medium-hot. Remove the cake carefully from the oven and spread the topping over the top, making sure that all the cake is covered. Place under the grill until the topping is golden brown, watching that the sides of the cake don't burn. Stand the tin on a rack so that air can pass underneath, and leave to cool before carefully removing the cake from the tin.

Serves 10

50g/2oz/4 tbsp unsalted butter, plus extra for greasing

115g/4oz/1 cup plain (all-purpose) flour

7.5ml/1½ tsp baking powder

pinch of salt

2 large eggs

150g/5oz/¾ cup caster (superfine) sugar

For the topping

115g/4oz/½ cup butter, softened

150g/5oz/1¼ cups blanched almonds, toasted and roughly chopped

115g/4oz/generous ½ cup caster sugar

30ml/2 tbsp plain flour

30ml/2 tbsp single (light) cream or milk

Cook's tips

• Tosca cake can be eaten plain with coffee or tea, or served with vanilla ice cream or custard.

• Another idea is to use the tosca topping to glaze canned pears before baking them in the oven and serving with whipped cream.

Per portion Energy 389kcal/1626kJ; Protein 6.1g; Carbohydrate 40.2g, of which sugars 28.7g; Fat 23g, of which saturates 10g; Cholesterol 75mg; Calcium 82mg; Fibre 1.5g; Sodium 119mg.

Serves 15

250g/9oz/2¼ cups unblanched almonds

250g/9oz/2¼ cups blanched almonds

500g/1¼lb/5 cups icing (confectioners') sugar

3 egg whites

For the icing

200g/7oz/1¾ cups icing sugar

1 egg white

Cook's tip As a finishing touch, it is traditional to stick little Norwegian flags into the celebration cake.

Norwegian celebration ring cake
Kransekake

This cake is traditionally used for weddings or other special celebrations and a well-made kransekake is an impressive sight. It is made from a series of baked almond rings, carefully graded in size. Sets of moulds can be bought in Norway that ensure each ring is the correct size to pile on top of each other to create a graduated cone, but you can also make them using circles drawn on baking parchment. Cakes can be made from 17, 18 or even more rings. The following recipe allows for about 16 rings.

1 Put the unblanched and blanched almonds in a food processor and mix until finely ground. Add the icing sugar and grind again. Add sufficient egg white to make a firm dough. If too moist, add more sugar or if not moist enough, add a little extra egg white.

2 Put the dough in a frying pan over a low heat and knead the dough in the pan until it is almost too hot to handle. Remove from the heat, cover and set aside for 10 minutes.

3 Preheat the oven to 200°C/400°F/Gas 6. Grease a set of Norwegian ring-shaped moulds with unsalted butter. If moulds are not available, draw a series of circles on baking parchment as a guide to forming the rings. Make the first circle 6cm/2½in in diameter and each successive circle an additional 1cm/½in. In total you need 16 circles. You should be able to fit several of the rings, especially the smaller ones, on one baking sheet. The rings do not spread very much in baking but allow plenty of room between so they run no danger of touching.

4 Roll out small quantities of the dough into sausage shapes 1cm/½in thick and make into circles to fit the ring moulds or the drawn shapes. Bake in the oven for 12–15 minutes until the rings are golden brown, firm on the outside and chewy inside. They should not be overcooked. Leave in the ring moulds to cool slightly, then remove carefully and place on a wire rack.

5 Put the icing sugar and egg white in a bowl and mix them together to make a firm icing that will stick the rings together. Using the icing, glue the rings together, starting with the largest at the bottom, placed on a large serving plate or board.

6 Pipe the icing in zigzags up and down the cake to decorate. If you want to thin the icing slightly for decorating, then use a little brandy or white wine vinegar, but don't have it too thin or it will drip down the cone instead of remaining in zigzags.

Per portion Energy 391kcal/1642kJ; Protein 8g; Carbohydrate 51.1g, of which sugars 50.2g; Fat 18.6g, of which saturates 1.5g; Cholesterol 0mg; Calcium 105mg; Fibre 2.5g; Sodium 24mg.

Suppliers

Norway

Jakob & Johan Dybvik As
(bacalao specialist)
Tingstadvika 5
6035 Fiskarstrand
Tel: 00 47 7019 9980
Fax: 00 47 7019 9990
sales@baccala.com
www.bacalao.com

Norway Abroad
(mail-order food)
Henrik Ibsengate 100
0230 Oslo
Tel: 00 47 2212 3355
Fax: 00 47 2243 8877
www.norwayabroad.com

United Kingdom

Norwegian Church
(holds an annual food fair in
November with a wide range of
Norwegian ingredients)
1 Albion Street
London SE16 7JB
Tel: 020 7740 3900

Totally Swedish
(a Swedish food store, but one
that stocks many of the core
ingredients for Norwegian, and
other Scandinavian, cookery)
32 Crawford Street
London W1H 1LS
Tel: 020 7224 9300
info@totallyswedish.com
shop@totallyswedish.com

United States

Berolina Bakery Pastry Shop
(a wide range of specialist cakes,
pastries and fresh bread)
3421 Ocean View Blvd
Glendale, CA 91208
Tel: 001 (818) 249 6506

The Crown Bakery
133 Gold Star Blvd
Worcester, MA
Tel: 001 (508) 852-0746
www.thecrownbakery.com

Distinctively Sweden
(specialist foods from Sweden,
Norway, Denmark and Finland)
15 Messenger Street
Plainville, MA 02762
Tel: 001 (508) 643-2676
www.distinctivelysweden.com

Genuine Scandinavia, LLC.
(kitchenware and accessories)
958 Washington Street, #9
Denver, CO 80203
Tel: 001 (303) 318 0714
Sales@GenuineScandinavia.com
www.GenuineScandinavia.com

The Gift Chalet
(Scandinavian gifts and food)
8 Washington Street – Route 20
Auburn, MA 01501
Tel: 001 (508) 755-3028
www.giftchaletauburn.com

Nordic Fox
(restaurant featuring
Scandinavian foods)
10924 Paramount Blvd
Downey, CA 90241
Tel: 001 (562) 869 1414

Nordic House
3421 Telegraph Avenue
Oakland, CA 94609
Tel: 001 (510) 653-3882
pia@nordichouse.com
www.nordichouse.com

Norwill
(cookware, food and gifts)
1400 E Hillsboro Blvd #200
Deerfield Beach, FL 33441
Tel: 001 (954) 596 4506
Fax: 001 (954) 596 4509

Olson's Delicatessen
(Scandinavian foods and gifts)
5660 West Pico Blvd
Los Angeles, CA
Tel: 001 (323) 938 0742

Scandia Food & Gifts Inc.
(Scandinavian food and gifts)
30 High Street
Norwalk, CT 06851
Tel: 001 (203) 838 2087
scandia@webquill.com
www.scandiafood.com

Scandinavian Marketplace
PO Box 274, 218 Second Street
East, Hastings, MN 55033
Tel: 1-(800) 797-4319
steve@scandinavianmarket.com
www.scandinavianmarket.com

ScanSelect Inc.
(Scandinavian food and imports)
6719 15th Avenue NW
Seattle, Washington 98117
Tel: 001 (206) 784 7020
www.scanspecialties.com

Simply Scandinavian Foods
(Scandinavian food and pastries)
99 Exchange Street
Portland, ME 04101
Tel: 001 (207) 874 6759; 001
(877) 874 6759 (toll free)
info@simplyscandinavian.com
www.simplyscandinavian.com

Viking Village
(Norway online store directory)
217 Ferry Street
Easton, PA 18042
Tel: 001 (800) 397 7180
Fax: 001 (610) 559 7187
Viking.village@nni.com
www.vikingvillage.com

Wikström's Gourmet Food
(Scandinavian delicacies and
gourmet foods)
5247 North Clark Street
Chicago, IL 60640
Tel: 001 (773) 275 6100
sales@wikstromsgourmet.com
www.wikstromsgourmet.com

Index

Publisher's acknowledgements

The publishers would like to thank
the following for permission to
reproduce their images (t=top,
b=bottom, r=right): p6
nagelestock.com/Alamy; p7tr
blickwinkel/Alamy; p8 Arco
Images/Alamy; p9 Dave and
Sigrun Tollerton/Alamy; p10 Mary
Evans Picture Library/Alamy; p11b
blickwinkel/Alamy; p12 Leslie
Garland Picture Library/ Alamy;
p13t Brother Luck/Alamy; p13b
Mary Evans Picture Library; p14t
Adam Woolfitt/Corbis; p14b Adam
Woolfitt/Corbis; p15 WorldFoto/
Alamy. All other photographs
© Anness Publishing Ltd.
Thank you also to Simon
Daley for the concept design.

Author's acknowledgements

I need to thank the following for
their valuable assistance. Åase
Walker (who manages the
Norwegian Food Fair run each
November by the Norwegian
Church in London) and Vencke
Tatt have provided much useful
recipe, cookery and general food
information. The Lamb Fricasée
recipe is based on one from Åase.
Berit Scott has translated many
of the recipe titles. Eivind Haalien,
Einar Risvik and Oddvar Rønsen
have been very helpful with a
range of background information.